WI

A RENEWED CHALLENGE TO PRAY FOR AMERICA

DAVID BUTTS

PRAYERSHOP PUBLISHING

Terre Haute, Indiana

PrayerShop Publishing is the publishing arm of Harvest Prayer Ministries and the Church Prayer Leaders Network. Harvest Prayer Ministries exists to transform lives through teaching prayer.

Its online prayer store, prayershop.org has more than 300 prayer resources available for purchase.

ISBN: 978-1-935012-69-6

TABLE OF CONTENTS

OUR DESTINY

John Knox of Scotland was the founder of the Presbyterian Church and a powerful man of prayer. Queen Mary, often at odds with Knox, said she feared the prayers of John Knox. Can we learn to pray in such a way, and with such effectiveness, that those in our nation who oppose the Lord's ways come to say that they fear our prayers? That will happen only if we learn how to pray in the power of God's Holy Spirit.

Jeremiah 18:7-10 gives us great instruction about praying for nations.

> If at any time I announce that a nation or kingdom is to be uprooted, torn down and destroyed, and if that nation I warned repents of its evil, then I will relent and not inflict on it the disasters I had planned. And if at another time I announce that a nation or kingdom is to be built up and planted, and if it does evil in my sight and does not obey me, then I will reconsider the good I had intended to do for it.

God has a positive destiny in mind for every nation. Its fulfillment depends on repentance and prayer. It is time for Christians in America to begin to seriously intercede on behalf of our nation. This book is a call to the kind of prayer that can change the direction of a nation. Not merely, "God bless America," but "Lord, help us line up our prayers with your purposes."

Each chapter ends with a Prayer Point. As you begin this book, would you commit to, at the very least, pray that one simple point? My prayer is that the Holy Spirit would prompt you to pray much more than that and that through the prayers of the saints, we would begin to see transformation that is clearly an act of God spread across our land.

CHAPTER 1

IS THERE HOPE FOR AMERICA?

I t was a vote that was heard in heaven. Party platform wordings at political conventions rarely garner much attention. But at the 2012 Democratic National Convention, an amendment was raised to exclude God in the Democratic platform, and it received as many "no" voice votes as "ayes." After three attempts at passing this by voice vote, Convention Chairman and Los Angeles Mayor Antonio Villaraigosa ruled that the amendment passed, regardless of the large group of delegates who objected. Had God just been voted out of a major national party?

Don't take this as an attack on Democrats. That vote was just a visible expression of the rapid secularization of America in virtually every aspect of our national life. What began slowly in the 1960s with the removal of prayer from public schools has picked up speed through the decades and has now accelerated beyond what most thought possible. Christians, and others who hold to more traditional values, often feel like we're living in a different country than we were before.

Same-sex marriage is now the law of the land. Those who are undergoing sex-change operations and therapy are considered heroes. Opponents are considered haters and bigots. Disagreement is not allowed. What God says in His Word is not in the equation.

A mother's womb is still one of the most dangerous places for a child since the Supreme Court ruled in 1973 (Roe v. Wade) that women have the right to an abortion. Between 1973 and the beginning of 2016 more than 58 million children have been denied the right to birth. And now the Affordable Care Act is beginning to use government powers to force companies to provide the finances for abortions for employees and families, even when owners of those companies are morally opposed.

Terrorism that springs from a radical view of Islam touched our nation deeply on Sept. 11, 2001. The resulting war in Iraq cost thousands of American lives, and we still face the growing threat of ISIS at home and abroad. This, combined with the threat of a nuclear-armed Iran, has created an environment of fear and uncertainty in our country.

Racial division has been a problem for many years, but it seems to have reemerged as a flashpoint for violence and hatred. The war on poverty and the war on drugs are wars we have lost. Wars cannot be won when we don't know who the enemy is.

I could continue but I won't. The point is made. We are living in tough times. It's hard to know who to trust or turn to for help. Political candidates and parties make promises and break them before the end of an election cycle.

The great danger for us now is that we will lose hope. Many Christians are pretty much convinced that we're living in the last days, and we can't do anything about what is happening. No hope for change. I should say in all honesty, that I, too, believe that we are living in the last days. But I also have great hope. Not just for the coming of Jesus but for His followers bringing about change on this planet and specifically, in the United States.

Christian author and speaker Dutch Sheets shares that optimism in a recent blog post.

Some Christian leaders teach, usually from theological influences, that America will not awaken, turn back to God and recapture her spiritual destiny. Their eschatology doesn't allow for a "comeback"; for them, the apostasy must continue to worsen.

Many secular leaders also contend, often with an ideological fervor fueled by their personal desires, that this rebirth will never occur. "America has 'progressed' too far," they assert with smug satisfaction, "having left behind its antiquated, puritanistic ideals and outdated beliefs." These naysayers are, indeed, correct when they euphorically and gloatingly bloviate about how far we as a nation have drifted from our original beliefs. Secularists and humanists are accurate when they condescendingly point out our moral shifts toward relativism and unbiblical values. With satisfied arrogance, these modernists gleefully vociferate that our government no longer sees itself under and accountable to an "imaginary" Creator, or even to an "outdated" Constitution He supposedly inspired.

With such a dire diagnosis, why, then, am I not hopeless? To the contrary, I have great hope for America because the depth of a fall never determines God's ability to restore. I'm not afraid of the powerful strongholds because size and strength are completely irrelevant when measuring His ability to deliver. And I'm not intimidated because statistical odds, whether of success or failure, cease to be relevant when God is involved. His limitless ability negates the very concept of "odds" and trumps all other winning hands."

Don't embrace any theology or creed that allows God to lose!

I have hope, and I'm dreaming. I dream of a reborn America that is once again a shining light to the rest of the world. I believe this dream was born in God's heart, embedded in a small group of emigrant pilgrims, and is one I am confident He still maintains. Join me as I dream. Partner with the "superintending providence" that was active in our founding, is involved with our present, and has great plans for our future.

Let it be said of our generation that when a nation teetered on the edge of destruction, having lost the ancient path of truth, we answered the divine call to war for its restoration. Let it be said of us, as it was of our forefathers, that in the face of overwhelming odds, we took our stand in the celestial courtroom, appealing to the Judge of all the earth for His saving grace, mercy, and sustaining power.

—June 16, 2015

Thank you, Dutch, for igniting a fire in many Christians regarding hope for the future. Without that hope, we will never give ourselves to prayer for our nation. The defeatist mentality, that says the best days of the United States are in the past, will not have the courage to pick up the weapon of intense intercession needed to face the challenges of our day.

THE NEED FOR HOPE

Hope-filled biblical focus is needed if we are to see a movement of prayer that moves the hand of God regarding the United States. Christians need to believe that God is not done with our nation and begin praying with passion according to the purposes of God. The focus of our hope must be in God and His Word.

If we look to our politicians, we will not have hope. If we look to our culture, we will lose our hope. If the economy is where we are placing out trust, hope will be lost with every downturn. Our hope must be in the Lord!

Scripture is filled with the command to hope in the Lord. Many times, that is directed to an individual for their own salvation. Sometimes though, it is directed to a nation. The Psalmist speaks to Israel with this powerful word,

> O Israel, hope in the LORD!
>> For with the LORD there is steadfast love,
>> and with him is plentiful redemption. (Ps. 130:7, ESV)

In a passage that I believe speaks much to our current situation, the author of Lamentations spends the first part of chapter 3 bemoaning the horrible situation that he is in. In verse 21 though, his thoughts turn to the mercies of God and he takes hope. Consider this powerful picture.

> "But this I call to mind,
>> and therefore I have hope:
> The steadfast love of the LORD never ceases;
>> his mercies never come to an end;
> they are new every morning;
>> great is your faithfulness.
> "The LORD is my portion," says my soul,
>> "therefore I will hope in him."
> The LORD is good to those who wait for him,
>> to the soul who seeks him.
> It is good that one should wait quietly
>> for the salvation of the LORD.
> It is good for a man that he bear
>> the yoke in his youth.
> Let him sit alone in silence
>> when it is laid on him;

let him put his mouth in the dust—
there may yet be hope" (Lam. 3:21-29 ESV)

Hope comes from a renewed focus on the Lord and his never-ending mercy and love. Lamentations points out the need of remembering that about the Lord ("this I call to mind," v. 21). There is also the powerful picture of humility and repentance before the Lord, "let him put his mouth in the dust."

A people who humbly come before the Lord, remembering His mercy, have great reason for hope.

In that great section of Zechariah 9 that combines promises of both the first and second coming of Christ, this insightful description is given regarding hope.

"Return to your fortress, O prisoners of hope;
even now I announce that I will restore twice as much to
you." (Zech. 9:12)

Those who await the work of the Lord are called prisoners of hope. That is a good description for the Church today as we long to see the Lord restore and renew His people, and with them, a nation that desperately needs His healing touch. Prisoners of hope never quit praying until the Lord accomplishes His purposes or until He silences their prayers.

PRAYER POINT

Ask the Lord to renew your hope regarding the future of the United States. Pray for a fresh vision of what can happen in this nation as we submit ourselves to the lordship of Christ.

CHAPTER 2

GOING BEYOND NATIONALISM

I've been in too many prayer meetings and gatherings where the prayer came wrapped in an American flag. You are never quite sure if it is the kingdom of heaven or the kingdom of Washington, D.C., that is being prayed for. I'm convinced that we will never be able to see all that God desires for our nation until we clearly draw a line and make sure we are, first of all, seeking His kingdom.

Please don't misunderstand me. I'm a patriot and proud to be an American. I'm privileged to travel overseas often, and as much as I enjoy visiting other nations, it is always a joy to step onto the shores of the United States. I'm old-fashioned enough that I still get choked up a bit at a well-sung "Star Spangled Banner." I love America!

The United States, however, is not a permanent institution. Like every other nation, it will serve its purpose and then join other nations in the delete file of history. That's not being fatalistic or defeatist; it is simply a clear understanding of human history and the history of nations.

The United States, however, is not a permanent institution. Like every other nation, it will serve its purpose and then join other nations in the delete file of history.

The purpose of the above paragraph is not to paralyze us into inactivity but to spur us on toward fulfilling our purpose. Our purpose is not to establish an empire, wealth, or wave our flag to declare how great we are. If our prayers are inwardly focused on ourselves and become only a way for a nationalistic pride to assert itself, those prayers will be unheard in heaven.

Until we have a clear picture of what we are praying for, I'm convinced our prayers will remain vague and powerless. Does God still have a purpose for the United States of America in spite of our turning from Him? How can we pray in a way that releases the power and purposes of God in our nation?

Psalm 85:9 gives a divine perspective on what God desires for a nation. "Surely his salvation is near those who fear him, that his glory may dwell in our land." God desires for his glory to dwell in our land. What an astonishing perspective! Especially when you consider that God's glory ultimately is His presence. God wants a nation in which His presence (glory) is welcome and sensed.

Now that is a compelling vision for passionate prayer! No longer a nebulous murmuring of "God bless America," but a cry for the presence of God to be known in the United States. Rather than a prideful assertion of the exceptionalism of America, it is a humble affirmation of the exceptionalism of God.

Some might want to argue at this point that Psalm 85 was an expression of prayer appropriate for the Jewish nation but not for other nations. Certainly many errors are made today by those who pull the commands and promises clearly intended for physical Israel out of context and try to apply them to current situations today. But Scripture is very clear that the Old Testament is written for us as well, and it is accurate to take principles of how God deals with people and nations from his actions toward Israel.

The Lord clearly desires for His glory to dwell in a nation where many of His people live. Regardless of which numbers you use, there are millions of followers of Jesus in the United States. God's purpose is for His glory to dwell in the United States, not to the exclusion of other nations, but alongside others who seek the same.

To help us focus our prayers on the purposes of God for our nation, we will need to understand what it means for God's glory to dwell in our land. Maybe the first part of that is what it *doesn't* mean. It doesn't mean a perfect nation. It doesn't mean a nation where everyone is Christian. It doesn't even mean a nation where every law is somehow based on the Bible. The only theocracy that God ever endorsed was in Israel almost 3,000 years ago.

Perhaps the best way to describe the glory of God dwelling in a nation is from the history of our own country. During at least three distinct periods, often known as the Great Awakenings, the glory (presence) of God dwelt in our nation. The stories from those days are compelling and tantalizing for us today. But we must also understand that there were many during these times who did not participate or even desire what was happening in revival.

As a matter of fact, during the Third Great Awakening, which began in September of 1857, the nation split right down the middle and the revival continued, in spite of the great suffering and trial of the Civil War. God's presence does not guarantee that everything goes smoothly. It could be argued that the Church was born on Pentecost in the midst of revival and difficult opposition and persecution. What we are seeking is the glory of God, not our own personal comfort.

THE GREAT AWAKENINGS

Read these stories of revival from our history and see how God's glory dwelt in our land.

1737—Northampton, MA
The First Great Awakening
Faced with a dead orthodoxy and declining churches throughout
the colonies, Jonathan Edwards and other church leaders began
to call for prayer. God heard their prayers and lit a fire of revival
that moved up and down the coast. In Northampton, MA, where
Edwards pastored, virtually everyone in town was awakened spiritually. The preaching of George Whitefield played a huge role in what
is often called the First Great Awakening.

1801—Cane Ridge, KY
The Second Great Awakening Begins
The years following the Revolutionary War saw a serious decline in
spiritual matters. Churches were closed and the new nation found
itself engulfed in crime, drunkenness, and violence. Once again,
Christian leaders began to cry out to God for revival. In response to
those prayers, the church began once again to experience the presence of Christ. In one of the more unique experiences of the day,
tens of thousands gathered at Cane Ridge, KY for a five-day camp
meeting that set the frontier ablaze spiritually! Denominational
barriers came down as thousands responded to the gospel and thousands more found their faith strengthened. The Second Great Awakening had begun!

1821-1844—Charles G. Finney
The Second Great Awakening Continues
Though part of the Second Great Awakening, Charles Grandison
Finney deserves his own section in the history of prayer and revival.
From the time of his conversion in 1821 until his death in 1875,
Finney's powerful preaching and revival focus led hundreds of thou-
sands to faith in Christ and many thousands more to experience

revival. One of the keys to Finney's success was the prayer ministry of two quiet prayer warriors, Clary and Nash, who would go to a community before Finney arrived and spend their days in intense intercession for revival. When Finney showed up, the ground had been prepared spiritually for a great harvest of souls.

1857—Jeremiah Lamphier
The Third Great Awakening/Layman's Prayer Awakening
By the 1850s, the power of the Second Great Awakening was waning. The U.S. was being torn apart by sectionalism, economic turmoil, and the debate over slavery. A young man by the name of Jeremiah Lamphier rented a room near Wall Street and invited businessmen to join him at noon for prayer. Six attended the first week, 20 the second, and within months, businesses were closed with signs on the door saying, "Gone to Prayer Meeting." This Third Great Awakening, often called the Layman's Prayer Awakening, brought hundreds of thousands into the kingdom and continued with mixed success even through the horrors of the Civil War.

1970—Asbury College, Wilmore, KY
A Regional Revival with Global Impact
Though the short-lived revival at Asbury College in Kentucky was very regional in scope, it has made a global impact. Beginning at a college chapel service one morning and lasting for almost a month, a revival of unending prayer, worship, and testimonies was the impetus for missionaries to be sent around the world, many of whom are continuing to make an impact to this day.

In chapter 10, we will look more closely at revival and how to pray for it, but for now, can we ask how we might pray in order to see God's glory dwell in our land?

PRAY FOR *FREEDOM*

It's really that simple. The word that thrilled our founding fathers and prompted sacrifices from them and many other generations down through history was freedom to seek God . . . or even the freedom to not seek Him.

In so many ways, the great crisis of our nation is the loss of freedom. The Pilgrims who first came to this country braved great difficulties because the government of England was not allowing them to worship as they believed was right. If Pilgrims were living today, they would be appalled at how that freedom has been eroded through the years.

It is not just religious liberty we are speaking of, though that is the one that strikes most closely to home as we consider revival. Other examples include unfair taxation, regulations in every area of life, and, especially dangerous, the stifling of free speech through an increasing pressure to conform to "politically correct" forms of thought and speech. In the name of "tolerance," an intolerant culture is taking away our hard-earned freedoms.

A rebirth of freedom in our land opens the door for the Church to cry out to God for His glory to come. Yes, that most certainly can still happen in the midst of oppression, but I believe the blessings of God can impact an entire nation that allows for the freedom to seek the Lord. One of the most important prayers you can pray is for a restoration of freedom.

The Bible is filled with references to freedom and has been an inspiration to millions through the years who have sought freedom. I would encourage you to pray through these passages of scripture often as you cry out to the Lord for increased freedom in the United States. Please note that some of these passages refer to freedom from the Old Testament law and others deal with freedom from sin. The principle of freedom however is clear. God wants us free to seek His

Face that His glory may dwell in our land.

Romans 8:21: "… that the creation itself will be liberated from its bondage to decay and brought into the freedom and glory of the children of God."

1 Corinthians 7:21: "Were you a slave when you were called? Don't let it trouble you—although if you can gain your freedom, do so."

2 Corinthians 3:17: "Now the Lord is the Spirit, and where the Spirit of the Lord is, there is freedom."

Galatians 2:4: "This matter arose because some false believers had infiltrated our ranks to spy on the freedom we have in Christ Jesus and to make us slaves."

Galatians 5:1: "For freedom Christ has set us free; stand firm therefore, and do not submit again to a yoke of slavery."

Galatians 5:13: "You, my brothers and sisters, were called to be free. But do not use your freedom to indulge the flesh; rather, serve one another humbly in love."

1 Peter 2:16: "Live as free people, but do not use your freedom as a cover-up for evil; live as God's slaves."

2 Peter 2:19: "They promise them freedom, while they themselves are slaves of depravity—for "people are slaves to whatever has mastered them.""

PRAYER POINT

Thank the Lord that He desires for His glory to dwell in the land. Pray for the freedom to cry out for that glory. Stand in the Name of Jesus against attempts to erode our freedom.

THE AWAY TEAM

In 2014, I was privileged to serve as president of the International Conference on Missions for the Independent Christian Churches/Churches of Christ. The theme I chose for our conference was "Vertical!" It was all about prayer . . . turning vertically toward God before we moved horizontally in ministry.

As much as I enjoyed that theme, I confess that my successor, Jim Tune, developed a theme that has grabbed my imagination in a unique way. His theme was "The Away Team." It was a powerful call to minister out of a position, not of cultural dominance, but of the humility that demonstrates that we really are aliens in this world (1 Peter 1). The "away team" mentality can have great impact on how we view our position in this nation and will change the way we pray.

Growing up in Indiana, I went to lots of basketball games. In the 1960s and 70s, most of our high schools were small schools that were passionate about their basketball teams. I remember the high level of excitement as we hosted other teams in our small gym at Garfield High School in Terre Haute, IN. It was packed with enthusiastic fans for every game. Even if it was a year with a mediocre team, the home team fans could "bring down the rafters" with our cheers for our team. The visiting team was the away team. They may actually have been a stronger basketball team, but we certainly had the advantage as the home team.

Home teams have the fans and the noise. Almost everyone in the stands was cheering for the home team. Often there was a small band that played the school fight song. Every call by the officials was cheered or booed by the crowd. It's pretty intimidating to walk into your opponent's gym as the away team. You always felt you had to not only play the home team, but the home crowd, and sometimes even the home officials.

NO LONGER THE HOME TEAM

For many years now, the Church has been the home team in America. We've had the advantages that a home team enjoys. We were the culturally dominant force that had to be dealt with by everyone else. When national leaders talked about faith, everyone knew they were referring to the Christian faith. People believed in freedom of religion and no one even considered such a thing as freedom *from* religion.

The home team advantage was enjoyed (and simply taken for granted) by the Church. Let me share a couple of personal, practical examples of how pervasive this was. In the 1970s, I worked on a mayoral campaign in my hometown. When our candidate won, I was privileged to sit in with the advisors who were helping the new mayor choose his staff. As we were preparing the press release for a man selected for a particular position, someone asked, "What church does he belong to?" When it was discovered he didn't belong to one, they turned to me as a young minister and said, "Well, you need to sign him up somewhere. He needs to be a church member." That's certainly not what it means to be a church member, but it illustrates the importance of church membership in those days.

A few years after that, I was working and preaching in a small town in central Illinois. The school superintendent called me, inquiring about our Wednesday night church activities. He told me that the school wanted to start an activity on Wednesday nights but wanted to make sure first that it wouldn't conflict with our schedule. That only happens when you are the home team.

The Church is no longer the home team in America. If we can understand that, we will pray differently and more effectively for our nation. So much of the conflict comes when we still act as though we are the home team. It would be pretty discouraging for a basketball team to come into a gym they believe to be their home and be met with boos instead of cheers. But when you know you're walking into an opponent's gym, you expect a negative response.

I understand how we can feel as though we lost something special. And in some ways, we have. But it wasn't necessarily good for us to be the home team. Remember my political friends who wanted me to get someone to be a member of a church so it looked good on the press release? In the same way, we so often had a watered-down, cultural faith that only vaguely resembled New Testament Christianity. Rather than longing for a comfortable memory, we need to embrace our role as the away team, which better fits who Jesus said we are. "Blessed are you when people hate you, when they exclude you and insult you and reject your name as evil, because of the Son of Man" (Luke 6:22).

An away team isn't trying to be loved and honored. They want to do their best to bring about victory. All too often, we forget that as we pray for the United States. Our prayers are often more about returning the Church to a place of privilege than about seeing the gospel preached with transforming power. Clarity of vision will allow us to pray in accordance with the purposes of God.

> Our prayers are often more about returning the Church to a place of privilege than about seeing the gospel preached with transforming power. Clarity of vision will allow us to pray in accordance with the purposes of God.

Several years ago, my prayers for my nation shifted as a result of a message I heard by a young revivalist, Kyle Martin. We were both speakers for a conference in Texas, and I was listening to his message when one phrase he used grabbed my heart. Though I'd heard similar things before, when Kyle said that we were no longer living in a Christian nation and we had better begin to act like it, the Holy Spirit began a work in me right then. I pulled out my phone and began to write some notes based on what I was hearing.

I've worked for years with various mission organizations and missionaries and we often talked about how they must live and pray differently because they were in a non-Christian country. As I heard Kyle say we were no longer in a Christian nation, it hit me hard that we needed to develop that same mind-set that missionaries had for their cross-cultural work. So I began writing some quick thoughts on how we must live and pray in America. All of these can be fleshed out in greater detail, but this is just an overview.

A MISSIONARY MIND-SET IN A NON-CHRISTIAN CULTURE

- Come into the culture determined to know and understand the people with whom you live.
- Don't condemn and judge them for simply living out their own culture.
- Bring the love of Christ into every contact you have.

- Learn the language. Don't expect them to learn your language.
- Make sure you have the necessary prayer support for your ministry.
- Look for ways that God has already begun to manifest Himself in their culture.
- Look for strongholds of the enemy in their culture and begin to pray regarding those things.

There are certainly many other ways we can begin to view our culture from this missionary mind-set, but these will drastically change the way we minister and pray. Can you imagine a missionary coming into a new culture and the first thing he does is begin to point out everything that is wrong? That beginning marks the end of his effectiveness in bringing the gospel to that culture. It's a home team mentality with an away team reality.

It is time for the Church in America to develop good missionary strategies for reaching our own nation. We can no longer assume that most people understand our "Christian" language and terms. It is a serious error to believe that those living in our cities and towns even know who Jesus is. It is not enough to elect some Christian politicians; we must re-evangelize America!

Of all the New Testament writers, it is the apostle Peter who most clearly understands the "away team" lifestyle and who gives us great practical instruction for living effectively in a culture that is not our own. Listen to his words from various places within his first letter.

"Since you call on a Father who judges each person's work impartially, live out your time as foreigners here in reverent fear" (1:17).

"But you are a chosen people, a royal priesthood, a holy nation, God's special possession, that you may declare the praises of him who called you out of darkness into his wonderful light" (2:9).

"Dear friends, I urge you, as *foreigners and exiles* [the away team], to abstain from sinful desires, which wage war against your soul. Live such good lives among the pagans that, though they accuse you of doing wrong, they may see your good deeds and glorify God on the day he visits us (2:11-12, emphasis mine).

"Submit yourselves for the Lord's sake to every human authority: whether to the emperor, as the supreme authority, or to governors, who are sent by him to punish those who do wrong and to commend those who do right. For it is God's will that by doing good you should silence the ignorant talk of foolish people. Live as free people, but do not use your freedom as a cover-up for evil; live as God's slaves. Show proper respect to everyone, love the family of believers, fear God, honor the emperor" (2:13-17).

"Do not fear their threats[a]; do not be frightened. But in your hearts revere Christ as Lord. Always be prepared to give an answer to everyone who asks you to give the reason for the hope that you have. But do this with gentleness and respect, keeping a clear conscience, so that those who speak maliciously against your good behavior in Christ may be ashamed of their slander" (3:14b-16).

"The end of all things is near. Therefore be alert and of sober mind so that you may pray" (4:7).

"If you suffer as a Christian, do not be ashamed, but praise God that you bear that name" (4:16).

What an amazing compilation of verses that speak to believers in the United States today! We certainly cannot begin to call what we are experiencing persecution without watering down the term when we compare our situation to the situation of many of our brothers and sisters in Christ in other places. But we are certainly no longer the home team and are discovering the inconveniences of being an away team. Speaking directly to us as the away team, Peter gives us wonderful instruction for living a victorious life.

Do you see how developing the "away team" mentality allows us to tone down the culture war animosities and instead become loving missionaries to our own nation? Our prayers become less angry and nationalistic and more loving and kingdom-focused. Rather than wanting the Church to be the dominant force in society, we want to see Jesus recognized as Lord in every aspect of life.

PRAYER POINT

Thank the Lord that He has called us to be His "away team" on this planet. Ask Him to give us the wisdom and patience to represent Him with grace and truth and power in our nation.

CHAPTER 4

THE UNITED STATES AND WORLD EVANGELISM

My friends in Australia keep calling me. I don't really know them. We've never met face-to-face, but we've been on the phone several times and more often, online. Why are they calling? Because they feel called to pray for the United States. And that's not just true of Australian Christians. Christians around the world have shared with me their passion and calling from God to pray for our nation.

So often the reason they give for their call to pray for us is the realization of how God has and continues to use the United States as a sending base for world evangelism.

Don't misunderstand my intention here. This is not mere nationalistic pride. The Church in America could have done much better with God's blessing of great wealth over us. We've not always had a clear vision of how we can better share our faith with the world. And yes, there have been times in the past when we have made the serious error of seeing our mission effort as making more Christians who look and act like Americans and ignoring cultural and national distinctions.

In spite of our shortcomings, God has used the American Church to spread the gospel throughout the world! And that fact alone may be what has stayed His hand of judgment regarding our sins. There has been a holy, God-given desire to see the message of

Jesus Christ taken to the ends of the earth and many, many Christians in the United States have sacrificed to go, while many others have stood behind them in prayer and provision.

I have often thought of a conversation I had in a hospital with a dear saint who was ill. She was a bit down over the fact that her grandchildren were not able to visit her. Her daughter had married a missionary many years earlier, and they and their children were currently living in Thailand. She told me I'd have to stand in for her grandsons that day. Glad to do so, I thought of the sacrifice of this wonderful lady and so many like her, who gave up the joys of the nearness of family so that the gospel could spread across the nations. God honors such sacrifice.

Understanding how the American Church has taken leadership in world evangelism helps us know how we must pray for our nation and specifically for the Church in the United States. The past missions effort of the American Church puts us firmly in the center of God's purposes for the whole Church in these days.

PRAYING CHRISTIANS

As we pray for the Church to continue to be faithful in this way, I believe we can still find ourselves with a place in the plan of God.

When the disciples asked Jesus what the sign of His coming and of the end of the age would be in Matthew 24:3, he gave an answer that culminated in *THE* sign in verse 14, "And this gospel of the kingdom will be preached in the whole world as a testimony to all nations, and then the end will come."

In 1973, Derek Prince spoke of this and related it to the Church in America and our vital role in the work of God.

For the final outworking of His purposes, God is thus bringing together the various resources that are needed: the human resources of Spirit-filled young people, and the material resources of wealth and technology. In both these respects, the United States has a unique contribution to make. The first mass outpouring of the Holy Spirit upon today's youth has taken place in the United States and is still proceeding across the nation. At the same time, the financial and technological resources of the United States are the greatest in the modern world. The nation that first placed men on the moon is uniquely qualified to place the messengers of the kingdom Gospel in every nation on earth. By the combined offering of its resources—both human and material—for the worldwide proclamation of the kingdom Gospel, the United States will complete the thread of divine destiny that has run through its history for three and a half centuries.

This special purpose of God for the United States was born out of the fellowship of the pilgrims. The vision God gave them was for the restoration of the church. To this, they devoted themselves with labor and sacrifice, with prayer and fasting. Today those who share the pilgrims's vision can see its fulfillment approaching. The church of Jesus Christ stands poised to carry the Gospel of the kingdom to all nations on earth. Through the achievement of this final task the church will itself be brought to completion.

From the study of the Scriptures, the pilgrims learned two great truths which they in turn bequeathed to their spiritual descendants in their own and in other lands. First, the end-time purpose of God is the restoration and completion of the Church. Second, the source of power for the achievement of this purpose is united prayer and fasting.

—Derek Prince, *Shaping History through Prayer and Fasting*, pp. 214-215

When we think of praying for America, we typically think in terms of praying against the rise of evil and for protection. Those things are important and will be covered, but perhaps more importantly, we must pray for the American Church and its role in the purposes of God. We don't often embrace the idea that our history of effective and faithful missions outreach is one of the key factors in our nation's continued experience of the blessings of God.

PRAYER POINT

Thank the Lord for the many missionaries sent to the ends of the earth by the American Church. Ask Him to increase the passion and commitment of the Church to reach all nations with the Gospel of the Kingdom.

CHAPTER 5

HOW TO PRAY FOR AN ELECTION

Is positive change truly possible in our nation today?

In every election cycle, American Christians have amazing opportunities sandwiched between grave dangers. We are privileged to be a part of a nation of people who have the responsibility to choose their own leaders. For those believing that godly leaders are a source of blessing to a nation, elections provide us with great *opportunity*. However, when we begin to put our hope in leaders rather than in the Lord, we open ourselves up to *grave danger*.

God's Word is very clear about having an undivided heart, trusting only in the Lord. King David, the mighty warrior, says, "Some trust in chariots and some in horses, but we trust in the name of the LORD our God" (Ps. 20:7). Awareness of this verse can create a tension in the thinking Christian. Some have overreacted and rejected the political process completely. Such people will be less motivated to pray over the elections.

A balanced and biblical approach, however, allows us to fully participate in the electoral process without falling into improperly placed trust.

INVITING GOD INTO THE PROCESS

In Paul's teaching on prayer in 1 Timothy 2:1-4, one of the major thrusts is praying for those in authority. According to Paul's reasoning, we want good government that allows us to live "peaceful and quiet lives"—ultimately freeing us to evangelize those who are lost.

Paul would have been amazed that Christians could someday actually take part in selecting those leaders. I believe he would have been even more amazed (and appalled) that many of those Christians didn't even bother to get involved in selecting those leaders for the purposes of God to be fulfilled.

Praying for the electoral process is the first step in seeing the fulfillment of what Paul is writing about to Timothy. I don't believe we should wait for a leader to be selected before we move into obedient prayer for those in authority. In prayer, we invite the Lord into the process of electing those leaders who will ultimately allow us to lead "peaceful and quiet lives in all godliness and holiness" (v. 2).

So why pray for the elections? There are a number of compelling reasons:

- The Bible commands us to pray for those who are in leadership, which would include those who are vying to *become* leaders.
- Godly leaders can help slow the erosion of religious liberties in our land, providing an increased window of opportunity for the Church to pray and evangelize.
- The selection of leaders who understand and lead according to God's righteous standards can bring great blessing to a nation (Prov. 14:34).
- Scripture also says, "For lack of guidance a nation falls, but victory is won through many advisers" (Prov. 11:14). The determination of who leads our nation will also determine who advises that leader and how we are guided.

PRAYING FOR OUR NATION, THE ELECTIONS, AND THE CHURCH

The following prayer points cover seven major areas that relate to our national elections, as well as some current flash points.

Note that there are more prayer points regarding the Church than any other area. As the Church goes, so goes the nation. Judgment most certainly begins in the house of God (1 Pet. 4:17).

This prayer guide is loosely structured for multiple uses. Choose from the suggested topics according to your interest and the leading of the Spirit. An individual might pick out a few prayer points from each category and pray those daily. A group might choose to divide them all among its members and cover the entire guide at one gathering. Some families or individuals may want to pray from this guide for months leading up to the election—and perhaps even beyond. Allow the Lord to lead you as you pray.

1. Our Nation and the Issues It Faces

- Pray for the judges of this nation, that they will seek the wisdom that comes from above. "But the wisdom that comes from heaven is first of all pure; then peace-loving, considerate, submissive, full of mercy and good fruit, impartial and sincere" (James 3:17).

- Ask the Lord to thwart the efforts of those who would remove religious freedom from our nation. "It is for freedom that Christ has set us free. Stand firm, then, and do not let yourselves be burdened again by a yoke of slavery" (Gal. 5:1).

- Pray for truth to become valued again in American society. "Then you will know the truth, and the truth will set you free" (John 8:32).

- Pray that our nation will increasingly see that God is our only refuge in the midst of the troubles of this world. "God is our refuge and strength, an ever-present help in trouble" (Ps. 46:1).

- Pray for our judicial system and lawmakers—that justice for all, tempered by mercy and compassion, will guide our nation. "This is what the Lord Almighty said: 'Administer true justice; show mercy and compassion to one another'" (Zech. 7:9).

- Repent on behalf of our nation, because we have turned from making Scripture the basis of law, leaving behind wisdom and instead looking to ourselves for truth.

- "We all, like sheep, have gone astray, each of us has turned to our own way; and the LORD has laid on him the iniquity of us all" (Isa. 53:6).

- "Then the LORD said to me, 'The prophets are prophesying lies in my name. I have not sent them or appointed them or spoken to them. They are prophesying to you false visions, divinations, idolatries and the delusions of their own minds'" (Jer. 14:14).

- Ask the Lord to pour out a spirit of repentance on our nation, that we might become a nation committed to following His ways. "You will seek me and find me when you seek me with all your heart" (Jer. 29:13).

- Pray that the United States will repent of its corporate rejection of the Word of God as the basis of law. "How long will you who are simple love your simple ways? How long will mockers delight in mockery and fools hate knowledge? Repent at my rebuke! Then I will pour out my thoughts to you, I will make known to you my teachings" (Prov. 1:22-23).

- Pray that a holy fear of God will sweep across our nation, leading us back to a place of wisdom and walking in the Lord. "Who among you fears the Lord and obeys the word of his servant? Let the one who walks in the dark, who has no light, trust in the name of the Lord and rely on their God" (Isa. 50:10).

2. The Election Process

- Pray for wisdom for voters and a safe and fair election. "My son, do not let wisdom and understanding out of your sight, preserve sound judgment and discretion; they will be life for you, an ornament to grace your neck. Then you will go on your way in safety, and your foot will not stumble" (Prov. 3:21-23).

- Ask the Lord to remove those who might try to unjustly and illegally change the outcome of the voting. "I will make justice the measuring line and righteousness the plumb line; hail will sweep away your refuge, the lie, and water will overflow your hiding place" (Isa. 28:17).

- Pray for a huge turnout of voters who use wisdom in their decisions. "Get wisdom, get understanding; do not forget my words or turn away from them. Do not forsake wisdom, and she will protect you; love her, and she will watch over you" (Prov. 4:5-6).

- Pray for protection from any attacks from enemies that would prevent or delay the election. "Do not be afraid of them; the LORD your God himself will fight for you" (Deut. 3:22).

3. Candidates and Leaders

- Pray for the salvation of those who are in leadership of our nation. Ask the Lord to remove all envy and selfish ambition. "For where you have envy and selfish ambition, there you find disorder and every evil practice" (James 3:16).

- Pray that candidates will take brave stands for righteousness, even when it may not be well received.

- "Therefore put on the full armor of God, so that when the day of evil comes, you may be able to stand your ground, and after you have done everything, to stand. Stand firm then, with the belt of truth buckled around your waist, with the breastplate of righteousness in place" (Eph. 6:13-14).

- "If you do not stand firm in your faith, you will not stand at all" (Isa. 7:9b).

- Pray that their families will be protected from harm and unnecessary scrutiny. "You, LORD, will keep the needy safe and will protect us forever from the wicked, who freely strut about when what is vile is honored by the human race" (Ps. 12:7-8).

- Ask the Lord to surround them with godly advisors. "The fear of the LORD is the beginning of wisdom; all who follow his precepts have good understanding. To him belongs eternal praise" (Ps. 111:10).

- Pray that each candidate will focus on the issues we face as a nation—and not on personal attacks on other candidates. "If you bite and devour each other, watch out or you will be destroyed by each other" (Gal. 5:15).

4. The Church

- Pray for a spirit of humility in the Church and an outreach toward those whom the Bible calls the least among us. "In the same way, you who are younger, submit yourselves to your elders. All of you, clothe yourselves with humility toward one another, because, "God opposes the proud but shows favor to the humble" (1 Pet. 5:5).

- "But God will never forget the needy; the hope of the afflicted will never perish" (Ps. 9:18).

- "The King will reply, 'Truly I tell you, whatever you did for one of the least of these brothers and sisters of mine, you did for me'" (Matt. 25:40).

- Pray that the churches in your community and area will preach the gospel of Christ powerfully. "For I am not ashamed of the gospel, because it is the power of God that brings salvation to everyone who believes: first to the Jew, then to the Gentile" (Rom. 1:16).

- Thank the Lord for the freedom we have in Him and for the wisdom to understand that freedom. "You, my brothers and sisters, were called to be free. But do not use your freedom to indulge the flesh; rather, serve one another humbly in love" (Gal. 5:13).

- Pray for a spirit of consecration and holiness to come upon the Church in America.
  - ✛ "Joshua told the people, 'Consecrate yourselves, for tomorrow the Lord will do amazing things among you'" (Josh. 3:5).
  - ✛ "But just as he who called you is holy, so be holy in all you do" (1 Pet. 1:15).

- Pray for a spirit of compassion to come over the Church in this nation so that we will begin seriously to live out the life-style of Jesus in our communities. "Therefore if you have any encouragement from being united with Christ, if any comfort from his love, if any common sharing in the Spirit, if any tenderness and compassion, then make my joy complete by being like-minded, having the same love, being one in spirit and of one mind. Do nothing out of selfish ambition or vain conceit. Rather, in humility value others above yourselves, not looking to your own interests but each of you to the interests of the others" (Phil. 2:1–4).

- Ask the Lord to help strengthen the trumpet call to intensive prayer, so that it is heard throughout the Church in the United States.
  - ✛ "Therefore I want the men everywhere to pray, lifting up holy hands without anger or disputing" (1 Tim. 2:8).
  - ✛ "Pray continually" (1 Thess. 5:17).

- Ask the Lord to equip the Church to rise up with a strong prophetic voice for America. "Pray also for me, that whenever I speak, words may be given me so that I will fearlessly make known the mystery of the gospel" (Eph. 6:19).

• Pray for a spirit of repentance to fall upon the Church in America that would cause believers to turn back to God and seek Him. "God looks down from heaven on all mankind to see if there are any who understand, any who seek God" (Ps. 53:2).

• Pray for a spirit of courage to rise up within the Church, a commitment to enduring *whatever it takes* to see the fulfillment of God's purposes in our nation.
  ✛ "Be on your guard; stand firm in the faith; be courageous; be strong" (1 Cor. 16:13).
  ✛ "You became imitators of us and of the Lord, for you welcomed the message in the midst of severe suffering with the joy given by the Holy Spirit" (1 Thess. 1:6).

• Pray that the Church in America will so noticeably live in Christ's peace that His peace comes into the councils of our nation. "Let the peace of Christ rule in your hearts, since as members of one body you were called to peace. And be thankful" (Col. 3:15).

• Pray for a movement of the Spirit that creates a dramatic cultural transformation in the United States, bringing about a nation that has learned to put its hope in the Word of God. "Do not conform to the pattern of this world, but be transformed by the renewing of your mind. Then you will be able to test and approve what God's will is—his good, pleasing and perfect will" (Rom. 12:2).

• Ask the Lord to awaken the Church to the temporary nature of the nations and to the eternal nature of the reign of God.

✛ "But the wicked will perish: Though the LORD's enemies are like the flowers of the field, they will be consumed, they will go up in smoke" (Ps. 37:20).

✛ "But seek first his kingdom and his righteousness, and all these things will be given to you as well" (Matt. 6:33).

• Pray that courage born of wisdom will be given to Christians in places of leadership in government, the courts, and law schools across the nation so that they will stand for a godly basis for law.

✛ "Have I not commanded you? Be strong and courageous. Do not be afraid; do not be discouraged, for the LORD your God will be with you wherever you go" (Josh. 1:9).

✛ "Then I will teach transgressors your ways, so that sinners will turn back to you" (Ps. 51:13).

5. Media

• Pray for truth to be an established standard in our news media. "In your majesty ride forth victoriously in the cause of truth, humility and justice; let your right hand achieve awesome deeds" (Ps. 45:4).

• Pray that media bias will be replaced by fairness. "The King is mighty, he loves justice—you have established equity; in Jacob you have done what is just and right" (Ps. 99:4).

• "Do you rulers indeed speak justly? Do you judge people with equity?" (Ps. 58:1).

• Ask that Christianity will receive fair coverage in all reports. "Have I not written thirty sayings for you, sayings of counsel and knowledge, teaching you to be honest and to speak the truth, so that you bring back truthful reports to those you serve?" (Prov. 22:20-21).

6. Spiritual Warfare

• Ask for great awareness and discernment as we pray over the election. "When you go into battle in your own land against an enemy who is oppressing you, sound a blast on the trumpets. Then you will be remembered by the LORD your God and rescued from your enemies" (Num. 10:9).

• "Be very careful, then, how you live—not as unwise but as wise, making the most of every opportunity, because the days are evil. Therefore do not be foolish, but understand what the Lord's will is" (Eph. 5:15-17).

• Pray for physical protection for all candidates and their families throughout this campaign season. "May the LORD answer you when you are in distress; may the name of the God of Jacob protect you" (Ps. 20:1).

• "Whoever dwells in the shelter of the Most High will rest in the shadow of the Almighty" (Ps. 91:1).

• Beseech the Lord for a strong hedge of protection around the nation itself during this time of decision. "May your unfailing love be with us, LORD, even as we put our hope in you" (Ps. 33:22).

7. Revival

- Pray for another Great Awakening to sweep the nation as the Lord's people learn to humble themselves with a contrite spirit, and to tremble at the Word of the Lord. "'Has not my hand made all these things, and so they came into being?' declares the LORD. 'These are the ones I look on with favor: those who are humble and contrite in spirit, and who tremble at my word'" (Isa. 66:2).

- Ask the Lord to bring revival to the Church in America.
  - ✝ "Oh, that you would rend the heavens and come down, that the mountains would tremble before you! As when fire sets twigs ablaze and causes water to boil, come down to make your name known to your enemies and cause the nations to quake before you! For when you did awesome things that we did not expect, you came down, and the mountains trembled before you. Since ancient times no one has heard, no ear has perceived, no eye has seen any God besides you, who acts on behalf of those who wait for him" (Isa. 64:1-4).
  - ✝ Pray for the preachers of America to fearlessly proclaim the Word of God regarding sin and God's love. "But God demonstrates his own love for us in this: While we were still sinners, Christ died for us" (Rom. 5:8).
  - ✝ "In the presence of God and of Christ Jesus, who will judge the living and the dead, and in view of his appearing and his kingdom, I give you this charge: Preach the word; be prepared in season and out of season; correct, rebuke and encourage—with great patience and careful instruction. For the time will

come when people will not put up with sound doctrine. Instead, to suit their own desires, they will gather around them a great number of teachers to say what their itching ears want to hear" (2 Tim. 4:1-3).

FLASH POINTS FOR PRAYER

Listed below are areas of controversy, disagreement, division—and sometimes outright hostility—in our nation. Some would pick other issues than what I have listed here, but I believe we must pray with discernment and strength over at least these seven areas:

- The life of the unborn
- The nature of marriage and family
- Religious freedom
- The U.S. relationship with Israel
- The growing threat of terrorism and the fear and mistrust it brings
- Racism and its growing divisiveness
- The idolatry of tolerance—and the resulting intolerance for those who disagree with prevailing ideas. This issue greatly impacts the other flash points.

AMEN IS NOT THE END

Prayer rarely stops after the "*amen*." When we passionately cry out to God over any issue, we should, with integrity, also find ourselves praying, "and Lord, if there is any way You can use me to be an answer to this prayer, here I am." When we pray for an election, simple honesty will then require us to follow up our prayer by actually voting.

What about broadening the prayer effort beyond your own prayers? Why not start a short-term prayer gathering in your home for the 30 or 40 days before the election? Invite friends or those with similar passion to join you each week for a focused prayer meeting that asks God to intervene in our electoral process.

In a country with nearly 350 million people, it is very easy to feel as though one person is incapable of making a difference. That is false on many levels, particularly when we consider the power of prayer.

As we pray—even as *one* solitary person—we are teaming up with the Creator of the universe to change situations. The only way that positive change is *not* possible is when Christians refuse to pray!

CHAPTER 6

THE ROLE OF REPENTANCE

The main message from God to nations seems to be repent. That can be a difficult concept for us to comprehend. We know the importance of repentance to an individual. As my friend, Richard Owen Roberts, writes, "Repentance is the first word of the gospel." When those gathered in Jerusalem on the day of Pentecost heard the first gospel message from Peter and asked how they might be saved, Peter's response was, "Repent and be baptized." We also know how important it is for believers to walk in repentance as we are made aware of our sin.

But why should a nation repent? And how do we repent as a nation? The spiritual principle appears to be that God only puts up with national sin for a season, and then He calls a nation to repent and turn from its sin. For those nations that do not know God, that season may last for even hundreds of years. For nations who have been blessed with a knowledge of God's ways, that season of forbearance is much shorter. He expects those who know Him to turn more quickly from sin.

God only puts up with national sin for a season, and then He calls a nation to repent and turn from its sin.

Nowhere is this principle so clearly seen as in Jeremiah 18:5-10.

> Then the word of the LORD came to me. He said, "Can I not
> do with you, Israel, as this potter does?" declares the LORD.
> "Like clay in the hand of the potter, so are you in my hand,
> Israel. If at any time I announce that a nation or kingdom is
> to be uprooted, torn down and destroyed, and if that nation I
> warned repents of its evil, then I will relent and not inflict on it
> the disaster I had planned. And if at another time I announce
> that a nation or kingdom is to be built up and planted, and if it
> does evil in my sight and does not obey me, then I will recon-
> sider the good I had intended to do for it."

God's hand of blessing or power to destroy is directly applied here to nations and sin. If a sinful nation repents and turns from sin, God will not destroy it. But a nation that is called by God to accomplish his purposes and instead moves into evil, God will destroy. It is interesting that although the Jeremiah 18 passage in its context is clearly talking about Israel, the way the Lord phrases it allows it to be used for any nation.

A good illustration of an ungodly nation that repented is the story of Nineveh and the prophet Jonah. After Jonah's brief side journey through the belly of a great fish, he came to Nineveh, home of the brutal Assyrian nation with God's message of judgment.

> Jonah began by going a day's journey into the city, proclaim-
> ing, "Forty more days and Nineveh will be overthrown." The
> Ninevites believed God. A fast was proclaimed, and all of
> them, from the greatest to the least, put on sackcloth.
>
> When Jonah's warning reached the king of Nineveh, he
> rose from his throne, took off his royal robes, covered himself

with sackcloth and sat down in the dust. This is the proclamation he issued in Nineveh:

"By the decree of the king and his nobles: Do not let
people or animals, herds or flocks, taste anything; do not let
them eat or drink. But let people and animals be covered with
sackcloth. Let everyone call urgently on God. Let them give up
their evil ways and their violence. Who knows? God may yet
relent and with compassion turn from his fierce anger so that
we will not perish" (Jon. 3:4-9).

Among ancient peoples, few were as feared as the violent Assyr-
ians whose capital city was Nineveh. Eventually, even pagans will
feel the wrath of God. But in this amazing story, repentance was
poured out upon the city, from the common people on up to the
king. God chose to stay His hand and judgment was averted for a
season. It is not by accident that Jonah records the dual response
of both common people and the king. As important as it is for the
populace of a nation to repent, so is the attitude and response of
those in national leadership. Would God have relented if the king
had not responded? Scripture doesn't say, but it clearly points out the
fact that the king did repent and called the nation to repentance.

CALLS TO REPENTANCE

The calls to repentance to the people of God in Israel/Judah were
many. Prophet after prophet came with the message that the nation
had turned from God and must repent and turn back. At various
times, the nation responded and revival broke out. Eventually, Israel
paid for continued unrepentant hearts by suffering destruction.
One of these calls to repentance that helps us today with its powerful principles is found in Joel 2:12-17:

"Even now," declares the LORD,
   "return to me with all your heart,
   with fasting and weeping and mourning."

Rend your heart
   and not your garments.
Return to the LORD your God,
   for he is gracious and compassionate,
slow to anger and abounding in love,
   and he relents from sending calamity.

Who knows? He may turn and relent
   and leave behind a blessing—
grain offerings and drink offerings
   for the LORD your God.

Blow the trumpet in Zion,
   declare a holy fast,
   call a sacred assembly.

Gather the people,
   consecrate the assembly;
bring together the elders,
   gather the children,
   those nursing at the breast.
Let the bridegroom leave his room
   and the bride her chamber.
Let the priests, who minister before the LORD,
   weep between the portico and the altar.
Let them say, "Spare your people, LORD.
   Do not make your inheritance an object of scorn,

a byword among the nations.

Why should they say among the peoples,

'Where is their God?'"

One thing that is clear from Joel; this call to repentance is not just an individual act, but a corporate one. This is a call to a nation. Blow trumpets; set up an assembly, invite everyone, from youngest to oldest; make sure your leaders (elders) are there; and above all, do it with your whole heart.

This is a picture of genuine remorse over sin from a vast cross section of the nation. There is no reason to believe that absolutely everyone from Israel was going to come. But it was a genuine response from huge numbers, and particularly from their leaders. This was not a small, unnoticed meeting of a few "religious" people. God was calling for a nation to turn around publicly.

REPENTANCE IN OUR NATION

Though it is hard to believe given our current secular mind-set, through the years, the United States has had numerous calls to repentance from our leaders, including presidents. God heard those cries and responded. The most famous of those calls is that given in 1863 by then President Abraham Lincoln in the midst of the Civil War. It would not take much to make the case that Lincoln had studied Joel as he wrote this proclamation.

By the President of the United States of America

A Proclamation

Whereas the Senate of the United States, devoutly recogniz-ing the supreme authority and just government of Almighty

God in all the affairs of men and of nations, has by a resolution requested the President to designate and set apart a day for national prayer and humiliation; and

Whereas it is the duty of nations as well as of men to own their dependence upon the overruling power of God, to confess their sins and transgressions in humble sorrow, yet with assured hope that genuine repentance will lead to mercy and pardon, and to recognize the sublime truth, announced in the Holy Scriptures and proven by all history, that those nations only are blessed whose God is the Lord;

And, insomuch as we know that by His divine law nations, like individuals, are subjected to punishments and chastisements in this world, may we not justly fear that the awful calamity of civil war which now desolates the land may be but a punishment inflicted upon us for our presumptuous sins, to the needful end of our national reformation as a whole people? We have been the recipients of the choicest bounties of Heaven; we have been preserved these many years in peace and prosperity; we have grown in numbers, wealth, and power as no other nation has ever grown. But we have forgotten God. We have forgotten the gracious hand which preserved us in peace and multiplied and enriched and strengthened us, and we have vainly imagined, in the deceitfulness of our hearts, that all these blessings were produced by some superior wisdom and virtue of our own. Intoxicated with unbroken success, we have become too self-sufficient to feel the necessity of redeeming and preserving grace, too proud to pray to the God that made us.

It behooves us, then, to humble ourselves before the offended Power, to confess our national sins, and to pray for clemency and forgiveness.

Now, therefore, in compliance with the request, and fully

concurring in the views of the Senate, I do by this my proclamation designate and set apart Thursday, the 30th day of April,
1863, as a day of national humiliation, fasting, and prayer. And
I do hereby request all the people to abstain on that day from
their ordinary secular pursuits, and to unite at their several
places of public worship and their respective homes in keeping
the day holy to the Lord and devoted to the humble discharge
of the religious duties proper to that solemn occasion.

All this being done in sincerity and truth, let us then rest
humbly in the hope authorized by the divine teachings that the
united cry of the nation will be heard on high and answered
with blessings no less than the pardon of our national sins and
the restoration of our now divided and suffering country to its
former happy condition of unity and peace. In witness whereof
I have hereunto set my hand and caused the seal of the United
States to be affixed.

Done at the city of Washington, this 30th day of March,
A. D. 1863, and of the Independence of the United States the
eighty-seventh.

—Abraham Lincoln

President Lincoln held the view that only the mercy of God
could save the nation, mired as it was in war and hatred.
Toward the end of December 1862, Lincoln discussed with
Rev. Byron Sutherland, pastor of First Presbyterian, Washington D.C.- "The ways of God are mysterious and profound
beyond all comprehension - Who by searching can find Him
out?" God only knows the issue of this business. He has
destroyed nations from the map of history for their sins. Nev-
ertheless, my hopes prevail generally above my fears for our
Republic. The times are dark, the spirits of ruin are abroad in

all their power, and the mercy of God alone can save us."
—William Johnson, *Abraham Lincoln, The Christian*
(NY: Abingdon Press, 1913)

In 1798, President John Adams made a proclamation for a
national day of humiliation, fasting, and prayer, which reads, in part,

AS the safety and prosperity of nations ultimately and essen-
tially depend on the protection and blessing of Almighty God;
and the national acknowledgment of this truth is not only an
indispensable duty which the people owe to Him, but a duty
whose natural influence is favorable to the promotion of that
morality and piety, without which social happiness cannot
exist, nor the blessings of a free government be enjoyed; and as
this duty, at all times incumbent, is so especially in seasons of
difficulty and of danger, when existing or threatening calami-
ties, the just judgments of God against prevalent iniquity are
a loud call to repentance and reformation; and as the United
States of America are at present placed in a hazardous and
afflictive situation, by the unfriendly disposition, conduct and
demands of a foreign power, evinced by repeated refusals to
receive our messengers of reconciliation and peace, by depreda-
tions on our commerce, and the infliction of injuries on very
many of our fellow citizens, while engaged in their lawful business on the seas: —Under these considerations it has appeared
to me that the duty of imploring the mercy and benediction of
Heaven on our country, demands at this time a special attention from its inhabitants.

I HAVE therefore thought it fit to recommend, that Wednesday, the 9th day of May next be observed throughout the

United States, as a day of Solemn Humiliation, Fasting and Prayer; That the citizens of these states, abstaining on that day from their customary worldly occupations, offer their devout addresses to the Father of Mercies, agreeably to those forms or methods which they have severally adopted as the most suitable and becoming: That all religious congregations do, with the deepest humility, acknowledge before GOD the manifold sins and transgressions with which we are justly chargeable as individuals and as a nation; beseeching him, at the same time, of his infinite Grace, through the Redeemer of the world, freely to remit all our offences, and to incline us, by his holy spirit, to that sincere repentance and reformation which may afford us reason to hope for his inestimable favor and heavenly benediction; That it be made the subject of particular and earnest supplication, that our country may be protected from all the dangers which threaten it; that our civil and religious privileges may be preserved inviolate, and perpetuated to the latest generations; that our public councils and magistrates may be especially enlightened and directed at this critical period; that the American people may be united in those bonds of amity and mutual confidence, and inspired with that vigor and fortitude by which they have in times past been so highly distinguished, and by which they have obtained such invaluable advantages: That the health of the inhabitants of our land may be preserved, and their agriculture, commerce, fisheries, arts and manufactures be blessed and prospered: That the principles of genuine piety and sound morality may influence the minds and govern the lives of every description of our citizens; and that the blessings of peace, freedom, and pure religion may be speedily extended to all the nations of the earth.

—As printed in the *Columbian Centinel*, April 4, 1798

This proclamation was issued on March 23, 1798 declaring
May 9, 1798 the day of fasting for the nation.

As old historical documents, filled with antiquated language,
there is a tendency to glance at them and move on. Please stop and
go back and read carefully both of these proclamations. These and
many others from our nation's leaders were used by God to bless
the United States. They are filled with biblical truth that is relevant
today. Repentance is a critical need for America today!

Many Christians have been involved in times of corporate
repentance on behalf of our nation. My fear is that we often do this
in a perfunctory way that, so to speak, takes care of that "repentance
business." Then we can get on with everyday life and ministry. But
at least they have done that; most Christians have not repented on
behalf of their nation in any way, and most certainly not in any
public way.

Until we humble ourselves and pray, and turn from our wicked
ways, and seek His face (1 Chron. 7:14), we should have no expec-
tation that the Lord's healing power will be poured out upon our
land. If the majority of Christians in the United States are not willing to respond to the call of Joel, I see no hope for our land. As for
numbers, that is in the Lord's hands, but the number of Christians
who know the Lord are much less than what we might think, I'm
afraid. A national call to prayer and repentance on behalf of the
United States is very possible, if we are willing.

The second issue regarding national repentance relates to our
leaders, particularly our political leaders. As far as I can tell, though
there have been many presidential proclamations of prayer, there has
not been a presidential proclamation of repentance since Lincoln's in
1863. No wonder we are in trouble as a nation!

In spite of how you might feel about the current situation in

Washington, D.C., I believe there are two significant action steps you can take to help bring this nation to repentance. The first is to pray for our president and congress. Ask God to grab their hearts and turn them to Himself. Pray that the Lord will burden them with the situation we are in and show them the need for repentance. Pray that God will give them the courage to stand up and call for that which is certainly not politically correct in our current environment.

The second action step is to vote. If you believe the Word of God that repentance is the only thing that will stay or delay God's judgment on our nation and that leaders are critical to that, why would you not vote for godly leaders? There is no excuse. I would even say that you may well be bringing judgment on yourself and your household by failing to help select godly leaders who will call this nation to repentance. It's not that hard. Pray, understand where the candidates stand on the issues and measure it biblically, and vote!

There is one more aspect to repentance that is unique to the United States. We are a group of united, regional governments that we call states. Might not the God who desires to pour out mercy and not judgment listen to the call to repentance of a governor and legislature of a state? It is certainly easier for Christians to make an impact on a state level than on the national. Once again, we must pray for governors and legislators in our states and be sure that we are involved, at the very least, in every single election for those offices.

PRAYER POINT

Make a commitment to pray for our president every single week. Ask the Lord to give the president wisdom and righteousness.

CHAPTER 7

THE PROPHETIC ROLE
OF THE CHURCH

Reverend Billy Graham, arguably the most well-known and respected evangelical preacher of the last 50 years, said in a recently published commentary that America was "founded by men who believed in prayer" and that prayer can turn "the tide of history."

"Even though America is just as wicked as Sodom and Gomorrah ever were, and as deserving of the judgment of God, God would spare us if we were earnestly praying, with hearts that had been cleansed and washed by the blood of Christ," said Reverend Graham in his commentary for *Decision* magazine, published by the Billy Graham Evangelistic Association.

"The problems of the world will never be settled unless our national leaders go to God in prayer," he said. "If only they would discover the power and wisdom that there is in reliance upon God, we could soon see the solution to the grave problems that face the world!" That is a prophetic word to our nation.

The most common role of a prophet in both Old and New Testaments was to speak to the people a word from God. In our day, the Church must accept that it has a prophetic role in our nation. We must speak a word from God to America with both truth and love. Too often our desire to be accepted or even effective in our evangelism has kept us from clearly declaring God's Word to a nation that has turned its back on Him.

It is easy to confuse love and truth. Paul commands us to speak the truth in love. Truth without love can be harsh and even legalistic. Love without truth is fuzzy spirituality that leads nowhere. If we do not speak truth, we are not loving. It may seem that way, but failing to warn people of danger is in fact an indication of our lack of the real love that changes lives.

One of the best pictures of this was given to the prophet Ezekiel. God called him to be a watchman to His people and warn them. The Lord speaks in Ezekiel 33:3-6, saying,

> and he sees the sword coming against the land and blows the trumpet to warn the people, then if anyone hears the trumpet but does not heed the warning and the sword comes and takes their life, their blood will be on their own head. Since they heard the sound of the trumpet but did not heed the warning, their blood will be on their own head. If they had heeded the warning, they would have saved themselves. But if the watchman sees the sword coming and does not blow the trumpet to warn the people and the sword comes and takes someone's life, that person's life will be taken because of their sin, but I will hold the watchman accountable for their blood.

Warning a people of danger is a sign of love.

One of the most helpful pictures of the prophetic role is that of the watchman, referred to by Ezekiel and many others in the Bible. God has clearly called us to this place of watching, praying, and speaking. In my book, *Prayer and the End of Days*, I wrote the following about the tasks of a watchman:

- They are to watch and pray (Matt. 26:40-41)
- They are to be on guard constantly and so provide protection. "Arise, cry out in the night, as the watches of the night begin" (Lam. 2:19).
- They are to listen. Jeremiah 6:17 says, "I appointed watchmen over you and said, 'Listen to the sound of the trumpet.'"
- They are to warn. "Son of man, I have made you a watchman for the house of Israel; so hear the word I speak and give them warning from me" (Eze. 3:17).
- They are to call on the Lord. "I have posted watchmen on your walls . . . You who call on the Lord, give yourselves no rest" (Isa. 62:6).

Standing on the walls of our nation, watching, praying, and warning of coming danger: that's a powerful and instructive visual for the role of the Church in our nation today. Who else can do this, if not us? What group of people is reading the Word, seeking the heart of God, and paying attention to what is happening around us? As the foundations of our nation crumble before us (Psalm 11:3), we must not retreat into fear, a critical spirit, or timidity. To the walls of prayer!

THE WATCHMAN'S CALL TO PRAYER

Scripture makes it very clear that one of the primary responsibilities for watchmen is prayer.

> I have posted watchmen on your walls, Jerusalem;
>   they will never be silent day or night.
> You who call on the LORD,
>   give yourselves no rest,
> and give him no rest till he establishes Jerusalem

and makes her the praise of the earth. (Isa. 62:6-7)

To those confused or somehow turned off by the reference to
Jerusalem, remember that we must always be careful to discern
biblical usage. Jerusalem is an actual city with great significance,
both in the past and, I believe, today. But it is also used biblically
to refer to the purposes of God in coming to dwell in the midst of
His people (see Rev. 21:3). Isaiah is clearly calling the Lord's people
to pray with intense, unending effort until the purposes of God are
accomplished!

The prayer movement that God is birthing in this nation and
others is of the Isaiah 62 type. We are no longer praying just "fix-it"
prayers that make our life better but prayers that grab the attention
of heaven because they are prayed over issues clearly on the heart of
God. Not simply a few added lines to a "quiet time," Isaiah writes
of extraordinary prayer that is day and night and doesn't stop until
God's purposes are accomplished.

We are no longer praying just "fix-it" prayers that
make our life better but prayers that grab the attention of heaven because they are prayed over issues
clearly on the heart of God.

As the Church watches and prays, we will increasingly be made
aware of the dangers, both spiritual and physical, that are coming
upon our land. That awareness will cause us to take up the trumpet.
Blowing the trumpet is a picture of warning people of danger. Look
at some of the Old Testament passages that speak of this task.

"Shout it aloud, do not hold back.
    Raise your voice like a trumpet.
Declare to my people their rebellion
    and to the descendants of Jacob their sins." (Isa. 58:1)

"Put the trumpet to your lips!
    An eagle is over the house of the Lord
because the people have broken my covenant
    and rebelled against my law." (Hos. 8:1)

"Blow the trumpet in Zion,
    declare a holy fast,
    call a sacred assembly." (Joel 2:15)

"When a trumpet sounds in a city,
    do not the people tremble?
When disaster comes to a city,
    has not the Lord caused it?" (Amos 3:6)

Many readers will look at these passages in frustration, realizing they do not have the means or voice to warn a nation. But you can give warning where you are. You can speak to those in your sphere of influence about what you are seeing and what you believe the Lord is saying in our nation. It might be quiet conversations with neighbors or posts online to those whom you know and care about. Giving warning of coming danger does not always mean standing in the street and shouting. For most of us, it is lovingly letting others know what you believe is happening and how to prepare for that spiritually and maybe even physically.

Men of the tribe of Issachar in the Old Testament were described as those who understood the times and knew what Israel must do (see 1 Chron. 12:32). That is our role today. Understanding the times, but not leaving it at just understanding. It is also knowing what the people of God must do during those times. Perhaps a very practical prayer for the Church today is that God would make us as the sons of Issachar, understanding the times and knowing how to live in those times.

The first step for many of us is to pray this simple prayer: "Lord, please help me to understand the times in which I live. May I not be dependent upon others' opinions but always seek after Your accurate perspective of what is happening in my world."

Though God certainly can demonstrate His perspective to us without any sort of human input, my strong suggestion is that He works more often through knowledge than through lack of knowledge. By this I mean, we will be more likely to gain clarity about what God thinks if we are carefully and closely watching what is already happening in the world. When a working knowledge of world or national events is wed with the Spirit of God, the result is always more understanding.

Rather than watching the news or reading the newspaper and shaking your head over bad events, why not add a prayer for discernment to your watching and reading? As world events unfold, instead of submitting to despair or anger, seek the Lord's insight over what is occurring. The result will be an understanding of the times in which we live.

The biblical text, however, does not end with the men of Issachar merely understanding the times. They also knew what Israel should do. This adds wisdom to knowledge. Knowing information is one thing. Having the wisdom to know what to do with that knowledge is immensely valuable.

We live in troubled times where there is little understanding of the times. There is probably even less wisdom to know how to deal with those times. How should the people of God live in these days? What sort of direction should the church take in the midst of the confusion of our days? If we as the people of God do not even know who we are or where we are going, how can we speak with a strong prophetic voice to our society?

Jesus gave signs to help us understand where we are in the flow of history. These were not so much given as a prediction, but as awareness and a call to prayer and action. The entire chapters of Matthew 24-25 are signs, both of the destruction of Jerusalem by the Romans in 70 AD, as well as of his coming. The tendency of so many Christians is to blithely say, "Well, no one knows the day or hour so I'm not going to spend any time on that." That attitude somehow assumes that Jesus gave signs for no good reason.

It's not for prediction, but preparedness. Paul clearly teaches us, "But you, brothers and sisters, are not in darkness so that this day should surprise you like a thief. You are all children of the light and children of the day. We do not belong to the night or to the dark-ness. So then, let us not be like others, who are asleep, but let us be awake and sober" (1 Thess. 5:4-6).

Whether it is end times events that we face, or remedial judg-ments for our national sins, the watchman Church must not be unaware. The call is to watch and pray!

PRAYER POINT

Ask the Lord to make you a watchman on the wall of our nation. Ask Him for wisdom and insight on how to pray.

CHAPTER 8

THIS MEANS WAR!

In 1965, radio broadcaster Paul Harvey shared the following message on his radio program:

> If I were the devil . . . if I were the Prince of Darkness, I'd want to engulf the whole world in darkness. And I'd have a third of its real estate, and four-fifths of its population, but I wouldn't be happy until I had seized the ripest apple on the tree—Thee (America). So I'd set about however necessary to take over the United States. I'd subvert the churches first— I'd begin with a campaign of whispers. With the wisdom of a serpent, I would whisper to you as I whispered to Eve: "Do as you please."
> To the young, I would whisper that "The Bible is a myth." I would convince them that man created God instead of the other way around. I would confide that what's bad is good, and what's good is "square." And the old, I would teach to pray, after me, "Our Father, which art in Washington . . ."
>   And then I'd get organized. I'd educate authors in how to make lurid literature exciting, so that anything else would appear dull and uninteresting. I'd threaten TV with dirtier movies and vice versa. I'd pedal narcotics to whom I could.

I'd sell alcohol to ladies and gentlemen of distinction. I'd tranquilize the rest with pills.

If I were the devil, I'd soon have families that war with themselves, churches at war with themselves, and nations at war with themselves; until each in its turn was consumed. And with promises of higher ratings I'd have mesmerizing media fanning the flames. If I were the devil I would encourage schools to refine young intellects, but neglect to discipline emotions—just let those run wild, until before you knew it, you'd have to have drug-sniffing dogs and metal detectors at every schoolhouse door.

Within a decade, I'd have prisons overflowing, I'd have judges promoting pornography—soon I could evict God from the courthouse, then from the schoolhouse, and then from the houses of Congress. And in His own churches I would substitute psychology for religion, and deify science. I would lure priests and pastors into misusing boys and girls and church money. If I were the devil I'd make the symbols of Easter an egg and the symbol of Christmas a bottle.

If I were the devil, I'd take from those who have, and give to those wanted until I had killed the incentive of the ambitious. And what do you bet? I could get whole states to promote gambling as the way to get rich? I would caution against extremes and hard work, in patriotism, in moral conduct. I would convince the young that marriage is old-fashioned, that swinging is more fun, that what you see on the TV is the way to be. And thus I could undress you in public, and I could lure you into bed with diseases for which there is no cure. In other words, if I were the devil I'd just keep right on doing what he's doing.

— © by WND.com. Used with Permission

What seemed outlandish in 1965 is a tame description of the United States today. Radio broadcaster Paul Harvey sounds like a prophet from 50 years ago. He hit the nail on the head when he portrayed the downward slide in morality and ethics as a part of a grand scheme of the devil. There is an all-out attack on our nation from the enemy of our souls.

SATAN AND SPIRITUAL WARFARE

The Bible is very clear about the reality of Satan and of spiritual warfare. The apostle Paul writes in Ephesians 6:10-18,

> Finally, be strong in the Lord and in his mighty power. Put on the full armor of God, so that you can take your stand against the devil's schemes. For our struggle is not against flesh and blood, but against the rulers, against the authorities, against the powers of this dark world and against the spiritual forces of evil in the heavenly realms. Therefore, put on the full armor of God, so that when the day of evil comes, you may be able to stand your ground, and after you have done everything, to stand. Stand firm then, with the belt of truth buckled around your waist, with the breastplate of righteousness in place, and with your feet fitted with the readiness that comes from the gospel of peace. In addition to all this, take up the shield of faith, with which you can extinguish all the flaming arrows of the evil one. Take the helmet of salvation and the sword of the Spirit, which is the word of God. And pray in the Spirit on all occasions with all kinds of prayers and requests. With this in mind, be alert and always keep on praying for all the Lord's people.

An understanding of spiritual warfare will change the way we look at the history of nations and certainly will impact our prayer for America. Satan has always attempted, often successfully, to use nations to oppose the work of God. It's not insignificant that when Jesus was offered the nations by Satan in one of the temptations, he did not dispute Satan's right to give them.

Governments of fallen individuals naturally gravitate toward power and its misuse.

It would literally be another whole book in order to trace the many ways that Satan uses nations and governmental power to achieve his purpose of attacking the people of God. From the enslavement by Egypt, the Assyrian and Babylonian attacks and destruction, and Roman conquest, the Jews of the Old Testament faced a relentless enemy determined to destroy them. Of course, from New Testament days until the present, it could be argued that Satan has not stopped his hatred and persecution of the Jewish people. Sometimes he even used a corrupt king of Israel itself to bring about those purposes, such as in the time of Manasseh.

With the establishment of the Church, Satan had an additional target for his attacks. The Roman Empire became a fierce opponent of the faith, not so much because it was opposed to a new religion as such, but because this new faith refused to recognize the divinity of the emperor, which was seen as unpatriotic. Most Romans did not believe in the divinity of the men who were emperors, but paid lip service to it because it was a way to show loyalty to the governmental powers. Christianity was seen as a threat to the state, as indeed it was.

Constantine's personal acceptance of Christianity ended the official persecution, but not the government's sometimes brutal intervention on behalf of certain beliefs or church controversies. The subsequent blurred line between church and state opened the door for government intervention into the life of the Church for the rest of history. Most of the time that was an open door for Satan to bring about division, heresy, and sometimes outright destruction.

The last 100 years of history have seen the rise of godless totalitarian governments that Satan has used as instruments to attack the people of God. Communism in the Soviet Union and China, as well as other nations, brought about the deaths of millions. The Nazi regime in Germany not only targeted Jews for extinction but turned their attacks on Christians who resisted their agenda.

In our current struggle with Islamic terrorists, we often fail to remember the history of this violent religion that has targeted Jews and Christians for well over 1,000 years. Beginning in 622 AD, the Muslim faith has used religious war to conquer in the name of Allah. Governmental power in the name of Islam, often called a caliphate, has been a weapon in the hands of Satan. It is no accident that the goal of ISIS today is a worldwide caliphate that forces everyone to worship Allah.

Governmental power in the name of Islam, often called a caliphate, has been a weapon in the hands of Satan. It is no accident that the goal of ISIS today is a worldwide caliphate that forces everyone to worship Allah.

Regardless of the century, the government, or the false religion, it is apparent that the Church has a relentless enemy. The question for us as we pray for America is how that applies to our nation and the Church in our nation. To answer that, and to be able to pray with effectiveness, we need to look at the enemies' attacks from outside, as well as inside, the United States.

In many ways, attacks from outside are easier dealt with. Christians need to be diligent in giving prayerful attention to the news and particularly to reports regarding those who consider themselves our enemies. In today's world that certainly holds true for an Islamic terrorist group like ISIS. We must pray that God thwarts their plans for world conquest. The Lord knows their plans before they do and is certainly able to show people of prayer how to effectively pray against their evil plans.

> Throughout church history, God has used the prayers of believers to change the flow of events and alter what might have been. One of the more dramatic instances of this occurred during World War II and involved the small group of intercessors that gathered in Great Britain under the leadership of Rees Howell. Again and again, God led them to pray over particular battles and situations, many of which they could not have known about through their natural senses. In numerous situations, the Lord used their prayers to ensure victory and change human history.
>
> Obviously, in cases like this, the prayers by themselves did not bring about victory. Men and women in dangerous places fought fierce battles and some paid the ultimate price. But the prayers of Rees Howell and his band of intercessors brought the power of God into the battles and altered history. For further reading on this amazing story, I recommend Norman Grubb's book, *Rees Howell: Intercessor.*
>
> —*Prayer and the End of Days*, pp. 22-23

THE NEED FOR MORAL PEOPLE

It is more difficult in many ways to pray about the ways that Satan attacks the people of God from within our own nation. It is an emotional issue and sometimes very difficult to discern exactly what is

THIS MEANS WAR! **73**

happening. The dangers emerge from governmental control issues as well as cultural shifts. Remember, Satan is very adept at maneuvering into control of human government and then turning it into a tool of his own purposes. He has done this for thousands of years in countless nations.

Our very wise founding fathers were very aware of the potential despotic nature of any government and set up as many checks and balances as they could for the protection of the liberties they held dear. They also, though, saw the need for the people themselves to be of a moral nature if this great experiment were to work. President John Adams wrote in his Oct. 11, 1798 address to the military,

> We have no government armed with power capable of contend-
> ing with human passions unbridled by morality and religion.
> Avarice, ambition, revenge or gallantry, would break the stron-
> gest cords of our Constitution as a whale goes through a net.
> Our Constitution was made only for a moral and religious
> people. It is wholly inadequate to the government of any other.

Fifty years later, Robert Winthrop, Speaker of the House of Representatives from 1847-49, wrote:

> Men, in a word, must necessarily be controlled either by a
> power within them, or by a power without them; either by the
> Word of God, or by the strong arm of man; either by the Bible
> or the bayonet.

It is at this point that the battle for the soul of our culture intersects with the battle for the nature and extent of our government. For almost 100 years, we have seen the shift in the United States from widespread acceptance of the Bible as the source of truth to a nation who, by and large, has no standard for truth other than the latest poll. Though men have always done wrong things, they still have recognized what was right. Today, the very issue of there being a right or wrong is debated.

Our universities, school systems, media, arts, and, even to a certain extent, the Church have been impacted by this relativistic worldview that dismisses biblical truth and standards. Over the years this worldview has made its way into our government, including the courts. No longer do courts or legislators look to the Bible for guidance. The result of this is a government that increasingly adapts itself to the desires of its people to be taken care of. "Protect us, provide for us, meet all our needs," seems to be the message of America to its government, and any government will be glad to be obliging, for with this role comes great power.

With the accuracy of hindsight, we can see how the Church allowed this to happen. All too many Bible-believing Christians developed a protective, insulating mindset that caused them to withdraw from the greater cultural influencers such as universities, arts, media, and even government.

Abandoned by the faithful Church, those influencers developed without the transforming power of the truth of Scripture and have produced generations who no longer believe in absolute truth. Certainly, there were Christians who stayed in those places of influence, but their numbers were insufficient.

Jesus spoke of Satan's disregard for truth in John 8:44: "You belong to your father, the devil, and you want to carry out your father's desires. He was a murderer from the beginning, not holding to the truth, for there is no truth in him. When he lies, he speaks his native language, for he is a liar and the father of lies." When a culture denies the very existence of truth, you are watching a culture that is being influenced by Satan.

Prayer for truth is a powerful warfare prayer. Praying for truth in our halls of justice, in the halls of Congress, in the White House, in the media, and in our culture is doing battle on behalf of the Lord. Asking the Lord to reveal truth causes the father of lies, the devil, to flee. The devil cannot bear truth. He knows that "the truth will set you free."

It is time for a militant Church to stand up in prayer and fight for truth. That will involve praying for those brothers and sisters who are contending for truth on university campuses, school campuses, in Hollywood and in the media, as well as those in government. This is a call to a different sort of prayer. Yes, we can continue to ask for our own needs, but we must shift our focus to our Commander in Chief in heaven. From Him we receive our prayer orders and begin to pray His truth and His Word over our nation.

PRAYER POINT

Ask the Lord to help you to love His truth even more and for Him to help you begin to passionately pray for a tsunami of truth to overwhelm every part of American culture.

CHAPTER 9

THE HOPE OF REVIVAL

here is not much to see at the corner of Fulton, Williams and Ann Streets in New York City now. Just three blocks from the site of the former World Trade Center, there is nothing that identifies this intersection from any other—unless, of course, you know its history.

About 158 years ago, God chose a small church at this intersection to begin a revival that swept through this nation and around the globe. Often known as the Third Great Awakening or the Layman's Prayer Revival, a prayer meeting on September 23, 1857, began a spiritual fire that brought more than one million people into the kingdom of Christ and saw sweeping cultural advances in spite of the Civil War being fought in the midst of it.

Perhaps it is more accurate to say that God chose a man, rather than a church. His name was Jeremiah Lanphier. Formerly a businessman, Lanphier became a lay missionary, focusing his efforts on New York City. In 1857, unemployment was a major problem, with 50,000 men idle in New York City alone. The nation was facing a most serious crisis with sectional divisions over slavery and economic policy. The power of the Second Great Awakening had waned in most places and the Church seemed powerless to respond to the needs of the nation.

At this critical point in history came a man with a simple idea:

gather businessmen at noon to pray for the city and nation. Lanphier put up posters around the Financial District of New York City and then went to pray on September 23 at the appointed noon hour. For 20 minutes, he prayed alone. Finally, five other men joined him. At the conclusion of the meeting, they encouraged him to do it again the next week. Twenty men joined in that following week. Within a few short weeks, thousands of businessmen and others were joining together to seek the face of God. The revival had begun!

It was not a revival that featured great preachers. Ordinary Christians gathered around the nation to pray, read Scripture, sing, and testify. The power of their changed lives began drawing their unbelieving friends and co-workers to the Lord. Transformed lives began to seek solutions to the issues that faced society.

Visiting that site on Fulton Street a few years ago, a fellow prayer leader and friend, Dana Olson, joined me as we stood at that historic intersection where God manifested Himself 158 years ago and prayed that God would do it again . . . in our day . . . in New York City . . . and around the globe. We walked and prayed and offered ourselves to the Lord as instruments in His hand. The Lord led us to pray Habakkuk 3:2 over that place and our nation: "Lord, I have heard of Your fame; I stand in awe of Your deeds, O Lord. Renew them in our day, in our time make them known; in wrath remember mercy."

Is there value in remembering a past move of God such as what happened on Fulton Street? The biblical record certainly appears to validate such an effort. Many times the Israelites were told to recall their history and find courage and hope in past events. In Isaiah 63, the prophet draws upon the life of Moses as he asks God why He is not acting in the same way in their day as in the days of Moses. The great prayer for revival in Isaiah 64 is based on a longing for God to return to Israel as He had been with them in the past.

Recounting the great acts of God in past revivals serves to stir the hearts of today's believers with hope toward such an awakening in our day. The act of remembering is not merely indicating an interest in spiritual history. It is a method, and a biblical one at that, by which we can create a longing within the Church for a fresh encounter with the Living God. Remembering past revivals can create opportunities for the hope for revival to enter into the awareness of the Body of Christ.

JOIN IN THE CALL

Would you join me in praying for a revival in the Church that will exceed anything that has occurred in the past? Will you ask God to visit Fulton Street again . . . and perhaps the street where you live as well? As you see how God has moved in history, will you pray with the prophet Habakkuk: "Lord, I have heard of your fame; I stand in awe of your deeds, Lord. Repeat them in our day, In our time make them known; in wrath remember mercy" (Hab. 3:2)?

I've been privileged to work with many key Christian leaders across this nation and more than ever before, I hear the same cry coming from all of them: The only thing that can save this nation is revival! If you are serious about praying for the United States, one of the most important things you can do is pray for a great spiritual awakening in the nation.

The Church is the key to the future of America. The nation doesn't believe that. We have been marginalized by culture. But not by God. As goes the Church, so goes the nation. Of course, that is true in a negative way as well as a positive, and much of the illness in the nation is the result of a weak and powerless Church.

> We fool ourselves to think that America can continue as the
> beacon of liberty and justice apart from the pursuit of the source

of liberty and justice: God. But while it's all too easy to lay the blame elsewhere for the problems our nation is facing, the truth is that it's the church that must step up. We have become too satisfied with the status quo—doing little beyond simply stating our concerns. But complacency does not become a people in pursuit of God. The church in America is in need of another spiritual great awakening if our nation is to survive the onslaught against her very foundations. This is not hyperbole but reality. Our nation's survival depends on the church's awakening."

—Alex McFarland, quoted in *Charisma* blog, January 6, 2015
"Impact of Great Awakenings in the Past"

What is this thing called revival? One way to describe it is a period of time in the life of the Church when the manifest presence of God is experienced and lives are transformed in extraordinary ways. Wikipedia describes it as: "A Christian revival, or revivalism, is increased spiritual interest or renewal in the life of a church congregation or society, with a local, national or global effect. This should be distinguished from the use of the term 'revival' to refer to an evangelistic meeting or series of meetings."

Revival impacts the Church or the individual Christian to begin to live the Christian life as God always intended. There is often a huge evangelistic result as Christians share their faith and as word of the revival spreads to unbelievers. A spiritual awakening is often used to describe revival that has spread beyond the Church and is transforming the culture.

Revival impacts the Church or the individual Christian to begin to live the Christian life as God always intended.

The United States has experienced a few Great Awakenings and a number of more regionalized revivals. Though not everyone agrees on the number, most would say there have been three Great Awakenings: 1730-1770; 1794-1830; 1857-59 (dates are approximations). I would place the Azusa Street Revival of 1906 and the subsequent launch of the Pentecostal movement in a separate category. Each of these not only strengthened the Church but brought significant changes into our culture. Looking at a few of the stories of these past revivals can give us hope for such a move of God in our day.

Let's revisit the earlier references to the Great Awakenings and see what else we can learn:

First Great Awakening

Concerts of prayer were organized because [George] Whitefield and Jonathan Edwards believed that if you have more people praying, then God is more pleased to answer. Prayer resulted in much conviction of sin. Some people said that hell opened before them, and they repented. Miners would come out of the mines, and they would hear Whitefield by the hundreds. Their tears made small rivers down their sooty cheeks as these miners came into the presence of God in repentance and faith.

One writer says that there was so much righteousness in those days that one could have left a bag of gold on the street overnight and it would have been there in the morning! There are some estimates that about fifty thousand people came to know Christ as Savior during this period of time. It was a genuine refreshing that God graciously granted the Church, reminding us that even the best of what man can do cannot equal what God does when He comes to a community.

When the revival was criticized, Jonathan Edwards wrote his book *Religious Affections* to distinguish between genuine and spurious religious experiences. Revival always breeds controversy because people want to know how to interpret what is happening. Satan works his counterfeits. But if we are going to pray for rain, we shouldn't complain about the mud. When we pray for revival, let's understand that revival isn't always the neat event we would like it to be. Revival needs good leadership to guide it. It needs good teaching.

—Erwin Lutzer, from a message delivered at the Heart Cry for Revival, April 2004, printed in *Herald of His Coming*, August 2015

Second and Third Great Awakenings
During the revivals and awakenings God has brought to this country, the impact in many geographic areas has been unusual. Often, God brought a special sense of His presence to a region. As a person approached a city, he could literally feel the presence of God there. Imagine then, whole areas of America so saturated with God, that you could literally sense God's presence!

During The Second Great Awakening (1794-1830), a divine influence seemed to pervade Utica and Rome, New York, during a season of revival. People would feel compelled to get right with God the moment they entered the city limits. So strong was this presence of God, that the term "zone of holiness" was coined to describe what was transpiring there.

During The Prayer Revival of 1857-1859, the Holy Spirit seemed to hang like a cloud over much of the East Coast. At times, the cloud seemed to extend out into the ocean. The following was reported by such a large and diverse number of people that the accounts cannot be doubted. Those on ships approaching the East Coast at times felt a solemn, holy influence even hundreds of miles from land. Revival began on one ship before it reached the coast. People on board began to feel the presence of God and a sense of their own sinfulness. The Holy Spirit convicted them and they began to pray. As the ship neared the harbor, the captain signaled, "Send a minister." Another commercial ship arrived in port with the captain, and every member of the crew converted in the last 150 miles of the journey. Ship after ship arrived in the ports of the East Coast with the same story: Passengers and crew were suddenly convicted of their sin and turned to Christ before they reached the American coast.

—Wesley Duewel, *Revival Fire*, pp. 133-34

Charles Finney said, "Many times great numbers of persons in a community will be clothed with this power, when the very atmosphere of the whole place seems to be charged with the life of God. Strangers coming into it and passing through the place will be instantly smitten with conviction of sin and in many instances, converted to Christ.

—Arthur Wallis, *The Day of Thy Power*, p. xx.

These stories about the "zones of holiness" are given in order to cast a vision for your prayer life. Wouldn't it be something if the "hell holes" of our inner cities and suburbs could become "zones of holiness?" Wouldn't it be something if America became a clean, vibrant, holy place? We cannot make it happen, but our God can! He has done it before! Would you join with me in asking . . . begging . . . imploring . . . pleading with our heavenly Father to bring a revival and awakening to our church and then to our land?

—Dale Schlafer, *Revival 101*, excerpted from
Herald of His Coming, April 2004

Third Great Awakening

Here is more information about what happened in the nation as the prayer meetings launched by Jeremiah Lanphier began to grow:

> Two days later, the Bank of Philadelphia failed. In October, the men began praying together daily; on October 10 the stock market crashed. The financial panic triggered a religious awakening, and people flocked to the prayer meetings. Within six months, 10,000 people were gathering daily for prayer in New York City alone.

THE MOVEMENT EXPLODES

Other cities also were experiencing a renewed interest in prayer. In Chicago, the Metropolitan Theater was filled every day with 2,000 people assembling for prayer. In Louisville, several thousand came to a Masonic temple for prayer each morning. Two thousand assembled for daily prayer in Cleveland, and the St. Louis churches were filled for months at a time. The newly formed YMCA also played an important role in holding prayer meetings and spreading the revival throughout the country.

WHEN MEDIA ACTUALLY HELPED

In February, 1858, Gordon Bennett of the *New York Herald* gave extensive coverage to the prayer meeting revival. Not to be outdone, the *New York Tribune* devoted an entire issue in April, 1858, to news of the revival. News of the revival quickly traveled westward by telegraph. This was the first revival in which the media played an important role in spreading the revival.

PRAYER EVERYWHERE

The prayer meetings were organized in the cities by lay people
and were interdenominational. Unlike earlier awakenings, prayer
rather than preaching was the main instrument of revival. Tents
were often set up as places where people could gather for prayer,
introducing a custom followed by later revivalists. The meetings
themselves were very informal—any person might pray, exhort,
lead in a song, or give a word of testimony, with a five-minute
limit placed on each speaker. In spite of the less structured
nature of the prayer meetings, they lacked the extreme emotion-
alism which some had criticized in earlier revivals.

—Diane Severance, Christianity.com

What is it we are asking for as we pray for revival? Ultimately,
it is for the people of God to begin to experience the presence of
Christ in a fresh new way. All other results flow from that. Changed
lives in the Church as well as transformation in a culture come not
from human effort, but the power of God made manifest in the lives
of His people.

This isn't about praying for a better life or that things would go
smoothly for us. It is about God and His purposes being accomplished. The acknowledged leader of the First Great Awakening,
Jonathan Edwards, was fired by his congregation in the midst of
the revival. On a much larger scale, as the Third Great Awakening
was taking place in the United States, the nation was dividing into
North and South and war then tore the nation into pieces.

Some look to another great awakening in this nation as the solution to all of our problems. That would be wonderful but unlikely. It
is more likely to take place in the midst of great difficulties and even
persecution. If it is widespread and lasting, it may well slow or delay
the judgment of God against our sinful nation.

More importantly, another great awakening can empower the Church to finish the task of world evangelization. All past revivals have had tremendous evangelistic outreach, and I believe the one to come will as well. In addition, the repentance and humility that will be occurring in the Body of Christ will be a key element in preparing the Bride for the Bridegroom. Revival in the Church can bring a restoration of New Testament purity, passion, and holiness.

How do we pray for revival? Certainly Psalm 85:4-7 gives us a clear picture and we would do well to use this in our own prayers.

> "Restore us again, God our Savior,
>   and put away your displeasure toward us.
> Will you be angry with us forever?
>   Will you prolong your anger through all generations?
> Will you not revive us again,
>   that your people may rejoice in you?
> Show us your unfailing love, LORD,
>   and grant us your salvation."

One of my personal favorites in revival praying is found in Isaiah 63-64. It is a long passage of Scripture that speaks of Israel's realization that they were missing the presence of God. They remember days in the past when that was not the case and cry out for God to come back to them. Taking this Old Testament passage and bringing it into New Testament realities is a powerful way of praying for revival. You will find yourself praying with Isaiah, "Oh, that you would rend the heavens and come down!"

As you commit to pray for revival, please don't keep it to yourself. Pray with others. Pray as a family for revival. Form groups to pray for revival. Encourage congregational and citywide prayer for revival. Consider using the National Prayer Accord as a model for consistent, persistent revival praying. America's National Prayer Committee and many other groups are encouraging Christians everywhere to develop this rhythm of prayer. The Accord calls for Christians to pray for revival:

- Weekly on their own or in small groups
- Monthly in their congregation
- Quarterly in gatherings of like-minded congregations
- Annually on a day like the National Day of Prayer (the first Thursday of May) or Cry Out America (Sept. 11).

The complete National Prayer Accord is in the Appendix in the back of this book.

PRAYER POINT

Thank the Lord for the way He has worked in revival in the past in our nation. Pray for Him to once again revive the Church in the United States.

CHAPTER 10

PRAYER THAT CHANGES A NATION

C learly, our nation is in desperate need of prayer. We need the power of God to be poured out. We need another great awakening. The Church needs to be revived. We need godly leaders in our nation. None of that will happen without prayer.

Most of us feel inadequate regarding having any real impact on a nation the size of the United States. But we believe God can change the very heart of a people. He won't, however, unless we ask. So it does come down to you. Quit complaining and whining about leaders in Washington, D.C., or your state capitol. It's time to pray!

How do you pray in a way that changes a nation? Many want to pray but don't know how.

Jehoshaphat was an Old Testament leader who prayed and led his people back to God. His story is found in 2 Chronicles 17. Though the entire chapter is helpful, I want to focus on verses 3-6:

> The Lord was with Jehoshaphat because he followed the ways
> of his father David before him. He did not consult the Baals
> but sought the God of his father and followed his commands
> rather than the practices of Israel. The Lord established the
> kingdom under his control; and all Judah brought gifts to
> Jehoshaphat, so that he had great wealth and honor. His heart

was devoted to the ways of the Lord; furthermore, he removed
the high places and the Asherah poles from Judah.

THE KEY

It ultimately is Christ we are looking for, not just a better nation.
We need a realignment of our hearts.

Jehoshaphat is a prime example of how beginning correctly
impacts a nation. There were many ungodly options for finding direction and leading the nation. Jehoshaphat clearly chose to seek God
and devoted himself to God's ways. As you read the rest of 2 Chronicles 17 and even the next few chapters, you see how God greatly
blessed the whole nation because the leader was seeking Him.

Jehoshaphat's seeking of the Lord led him to place the Scriptures in a place of honor in the life of his nation. He literally led the
way in making sure the people knew what was right and what was
wrong. In 2 Chronicles 19:4, Jehoshaphat went out himself into the
villages and led the people spiritually.

If you are reading this and saying, "Oh, I wish our leaders
would do this," my question to you is, "Are you asking God to raise
up political leaders who are also godly leaders?" Why not? James
tells us we do not have because we do not ask (4:3). You can make a
difference in the spiritual climate of our nation by praying for those
who are in office and those who are seeking office. Pray that they
would, like Jehoshaphat, first of all seek God!

But praying for leaders should not be a one-shot deal. We need
to press in with persistence. Christians are literally commanded in
1 Timothy 2:1-4 to pray for our leaders. Instead of complaining, we
need to be interceding.

I would also suggest that you personally begin to seek the Lord
with greater passion and intensity. It is not just our leaders who need

to draw near to CHRIST and experience His presence. Each one of us needs this. The promise of Scripture is that if you seek, you will find. We are told in the book of James that if we would draw near to Him, He would draw near to us. It is an absolute promise from the Lord!

... begin to seek the Lord with greater passion and intensity. It is not just our leaders who need to draw near to CHRIST and experience His presence. Each one of us needs this.

Imagine living in a nation where a large number of people are crying out to God for His presence and are passionately seeking Him. You will find yourself in a community where love is leading the way. Those who are hurting are helped by their neighbors rather than an impersonal government agency. Justice for all becomes a way of life rather than a catch-phrase. Peace is sought by all. It really can happen! But we must do our part and become a people of prayer.

We also need to pray about our follow-up actions. Jehoshaphat twice goes about the nation teaching the people to follow the Lord. Rarely is prayer the last thing we do. Often, prayer launches us into divinely inspired activity that the Lord uses to help answer our own prayers.

Things you might do to help with the direction of our nation:

- Work for a candidate.
- Run for office.
- Volunteer at a crisis pregnancy center or a place that feeds the hungry.

- Above all, become an active part of your church's efforts to reach your community for Christ.

I believe, along with many others, that God is not done with the United States. There is hope for another great awakening that honors the Lord and releases his power for transformation in our culture. Depending upon your viewpoint, it may well be the last revival before the Lord returns to bring this age to a close. I don't know about you, but I want to be in on what God is doing in our day. And without question, that means that we commit ourselves to become a people of prayer, prayer through which God works His purposes in our nation and around the world.

PRAYER POINT

Begin to passionately seek the Lord in greater ways in your own life and pray with that same passion for our political leaders to know the Lord.

THE NATIONAL PRAYER ACCORD

T he National Prayer Accord is patterned after a rhythm of prayer established by Jonathan Edwards and churches in the colonies prior to the First Great Awakening in the United States. In more recent days, many prayer and revival ministries are encouraging believers and churches to adopt this ongoing rhythm of prayer in their own circles.

In Recognition of:

- Our absolute dependence on God
- The moral and spiritual challenges facing our nation
- Our national need for repentance and divine intervention
- The covenants of prayer that God has answered throughout history
- Our great hope for a general awakening to the lordship of Christ, the unity of His Body, and the sovereignty of His Kingdom

We strongly urge all churches and followers of Jesus in America to unite in seeking the face of God through prayer and fasting, persistently asking our Father to send revival to the Church and spiritual awakening to our nation so that Christ's Great Commission might be fulfilled worldwide in our generation.

This voluntary agreement in prayer seems "good to the Holy Spirit and to us" (Acts 15:28) in light of the promise of Jesus in Matthew 18:19 and the unity for which Jesus prayed in John 17. This prayer accord presupposes a spirit of freedom to adjust its component parts as local Christians see need.

Though many are seeking God more often than this prayer accord outlines, calling millions of others around focused times of prayer is an urgent need.

We resolve to promote as an ongoing "Rhythm of Prayer" . . .

Weekly . . . In private or small group prayer, which lends itself to a focus on the regular preaching and teaching of God's Word, asking the Holy Spirit to light the fires of revival by anointing our preachers and teachers each week.

Monthly . . . In local ministry prayer gatherings, such as a midweek prayer meeting, a Bible study class, a Sunday evening service, a home group, or one meeting of a college campus group, etc. for the exclusive purpose of prayer for revival.

Quarterly . . . In prayer gatherings among local ministries and groups, uniting churches in a community, college ministries in the area, businessmen's groups, or radio listeners for an evening meeting, a luncheon, or a segment of airtime focusing on prayer for the community or region.

Annually . . . In prayer meetings designed to unite Christians nationally, such as the National Day of Prayer, the first Thursday of May, and Cry Out America, September 11 each year—occasions that call millions of people to pray together.

The National Prayer Committee and its partners offer tools,

templates, and stories to help facilitate this prayer accord (nationalprayeraccord.com), while recommending that other ministries do the same.

Downstream in America we find the symptoms and signs of church irrelevance, fragmented relationships, cultural decay, moral decline, and love growing cold, but Upstream from such symptoms, we find hope in united prevailing prayer.

- "… but I have prayed for you and when you are restored strengthen others" (Luke 22:32). As certainly as Jesus prayed for Peter, He prays for us!
- "Jesus Christ is the same yesterday and today, yes forever" (Hebrews 13:8).
- "He always lives to make intercession" (Hebrews 7:25).
- "Christ Jesus is He … who also intercedes for us" (Romans 8:33).

We resolve to promote as "Prayer Goals" the outpouring of God's Spirit for . . .

The Revival of the Church as Evidenced by the Indicators of Awakening in the Church:

1. Increasing testimony of the manifest presence of God.
2. Increased conversions and baptisms.
3. Amplified participation in corporate as well as individual prayer, fasting, and other spiritual disciplines leading to more effective discipleship.
4. A decrease in divorces and renewed commitment to marriage between a man and a woman in covenant relationship as God intends.

5. Imparting faith to children and youth as parents are equipped by the church to become primary disciplers of their children.

6. Among churches, a passionate pursuit for the well-being of their cities through the planting of new congregations, benevolent ministries, practical service, and focused evangelism.

7. Commitment to radical generosity as evidenced by compassion ministries and global missions.

8. Improved health among ministers as evidenced by their joy, decreased resignations, healthy loving relationships within their families, and an increased response among young people called to the ministry.

9. Christians involved in bold witness accompanied by miracles, dramatic conversions, and Holy Spirit empowered victories over evil.

10. Heightened expressions of love and unity among all believers, as demonstrated by the unity of pastors and leaders.

The Advancement of the Kingdom as Evidenced by These Indicators of Awakening in the Culture:

1. Breakdowns of racial, social, and status barriers as Christ's church celebrates together—Jesus!

2. A restoration of morality, ethical foundations and accountability among leaders of church and government, business and politics.

3. A transformation of society through the restoration of Christ's influence in the arts, media, and communications.

4. Increased care for the hungry and homeless, the most vulnerable and needy.

5. Young adults, students, and children embracing the claims and lifestyle of Christ through the witness of peers who live and love as Jesus.

6. Community and national leaders seeking out the church as an answer to society's problems.

7. Increased care for children as "gifts from the Lord" as the gospel addresses abortion, adoption, foster care, and child well-being.

8. Righteous relations between men and women: decrease in divorce rates, cohabitation, same-sex relations, sexual abuse, sexual trafficking, out-of-wedlock children, and STDs.

9. An awakening to the "fear of the Lord" rather than the approval of people, thus restoring integrity and credibility.

10. Neighborhood transformation and an accompanying decrease of social ills through increased expressions of "loving your neighbor" in service, compassion, and unity.

Developed by America's National Prayer Committee in partnership with OneCry and the Awakening America Alliance.

PRAYING FOR AMERICA
7-DAY PRAYER GUIDE

I am sure your desire to pray for the United States is heightened after reading *With One Cry*. This bonus section is a seven-day guide that will help get you started.

Each day has a Scripture, a devotional thought, some prayer points and a prayer. Let them stimulate you toward a deeper level of prayer for our nation.

This section is taken from *Desperate for Change: 40 Days of Prayer for America*, a prayer guide I wrote a few years ago. That resource is still available for purchase if you would like to be guided for a longer period of time.

DAY ONE

"The fear of the LORD is the beginning of knowledge, but fools despise wisdom and discipline." –Proverbs 1:7

This well-known passage of Scripture is typically used for individuals, and rightly so. The principle, however, can be applied to a whole nation. If a nation is characterized by the fear of the Lord in its dealings, both internally and internationally, it will be a nation known for wisdom and not foolishness.

A wise nation takes into account the Word of God as it makes laws. Even a cursory reading of the history of the founding of the United States demonstrates that our founding fathers seriously endeavored to base our nation's laws on their strong Judeo-Christian beliefs. Secularists today often counter that many of those men were, in fact, Deists, and not strong Christians. Their own beliefs aside, our Founders, almost to a man, insisted that laws were based on divine revelation and not on human wisdom alone. Even as strong a secularist as Thomas Jefferson said powerfully, "And can the liberties of a nation be thought secure when we have removed their only firm basis, a conviction in the minds of the people that these liberties are the gift of God? That they are not to be violated but with His wrath? Indeed I tremble for my country when I reflect that God is just: that His justice cannot sleep for ever." (Paul Leicester Ford, ed., *The Writings of Thomas Jefferson*, 10 vols., *Notes on the State of Virginia* (New York: G.P. Putnam's Sons, 1892-99), Query XVIII, 4:232.)

A significant shift has taken place in American political and cultural thought over the past fifty years, replacing God's Word as the source of morality, ethics, and law, with the rule of polls and surveys. This is exactly what Proverbs warns us against. A nation that rejects the Word of God as the basis for right and wrong has become a foolish nation that despises wisdom and rejects discipline.

PRAYER POINTS

• Pray that the United States will repent of its corporate rejection of the Word of God as the basis of law.

• Pray that a holy fear of God will sweep across our nation, leading us back to a place of wisdom.

• Pray that courage born of wisdom will be given to Christians in places of leadership in government, the courts, and law schools across the nation so that they will stand for a godly basis for law.

My Prayer

Father, I give You thanks for the godly foundation of my nation. Thank You for instilling the fear of the Lord into our Founders, so that our laws were based on Your Word. Imperfect though they were, the original documents of government for the United States made a real effort to reflect Your will and Your truth.

Forgive us for drifting from Your ways. We have turned from the fear of God to the fear of man. Our laws change with the shifting winds of human opinion. We have embraced foolishness and rejected Your discipline.

We confess our desperate need for Your truth once again to become the foundation for our country. Pour out a hunger for truth and righteousness on everyone from preachers to professors to presidents. Raise up a standard of righteousness across this nation that honors Your Word and exalts Your name!

DAY TWO

"The Lord is a refuge for the oppressed, a stronghold in times of trouble." –Psalm 9:9

If there was ever a nation that understood what it means to be a refuge for the oppressed, it ought to be the United States. The inscription from Emma Lazarus on the base of the Statue of Liberty has meant far more than words to millions. "Give me your tired, your poor, your huddled masses yearning to breathe free."

As a nation, by and large, comprised of immigrants and their descendants, many of whom were fleeing persecution or oppression in their own nations, we have been a land of refuge. The United States truly has been a stronghold in times of trouble for many.

Though this is a proud heritage and a significant part of who we are as a nation, we have always served as a refuge imperfectly. Some groups were more welcome than others. Some arrived and wondered if they were, in fact, better off here. We still struggle with what it means to open our national doors to others.

The good news is that the Lord is a perfect refuge, a perfect stronghold in times of trouble. He is a refuge, not only for individuals, but for a nation as well. When a nation turns to God, He will be a refuge for them. In the midst of the chaos of current events, whether it is financial collapse, terrorism, or war, how comforting to know that God wants to be a stronghold for our nation.

PRAYER POINTS

• Ask the Lord to turn the hearts of the citizens and leaders of the United States to Himself.

• Invite the Lord to be your refuge and your stronghold.
• Pray that our nation will increasingly see that God is our only refuge in the midst of the troubles of this world.

My Prayer

Father, I am so grateful that You are my refuge and stronghold. I come to You today longing more and more to experience Your Presence and to rest in Who You are. Show me more of what it means for You to be my refuge in the midst of the storms of this life.

What I ask for myself, I also ask for my nation. Help us not to trust in our finances, our technology, or our military might. Lord, You are our refuge, our stronghold in times of trouble. We come running to You, Lord! Forgive us of our self-sufficient spirit. We need You, Lord.

DAY THREE

"This is what the LORD Almighty says: 'Administer true justice; show mercy and compassion to one another.'" –Zechariah 7:9

As a schoolboy in the late 1950s and early 1960s, I remember starting every school day by reciting the Pledge of Allegiance. The constant repetition allows the words of the Pledge to be recalled effortlessly today, half a century later.

"I pledge allegiance to the flag of the United States of America, and to the republic for which it stands, one nation under God, indivisible, with liberty and justice for all."

Have you considered the fact that a nation committed to justice for all is a nation that God can bless? God is passionate about justice because it is in accordance with His nature to be just in all His dealings. When nations base their laws and institutions on principles of justice for all, the God of justice is pleased.

Of course, this means that the contrary is true as well. When injustice creeps in, it brings with it the displeasure of God. God especially seems to look out for the welfare of those whom society overlooks . . . the poor, the less-privileged, the stranger, and the outcast. The nation that wants the blessing of God will ensure justice for all!

PRAYER POINTS

• Thank the Lord that He is a God of justice and shows no favoritism.
• Thank God for a nation that proclaims itself a land of justice for all.
• Pray for our judicial system and lawmakers, that justice for all, tempered by mercy and compassion, will guide our nation.

My Prayer

I thank You, Lord, that You are perfectly just in all Your ways. You deal with us impartially, imparting justice while showing mercy and compassion. Help us to be like You in this way.

I'm grateful, Lord, that the United States has built justice into its very foundation. Forgive us when we have failed to carry out what we say we believe in. Help us as a nation to offer justice to all and not to discriminate in the way that justice is administered.

I pray for the judicial system of this nation. Restore godliness to the courts of our land. May those who make our laws do so with a deep commitment to justice for all. In the name of Jesus, we come against any spirit of privilege or special interests that would mar the true administration of justice. We cry out with the prophet Amos, "Let justice roll on like a river" (Amos 5:24). May a river of justice and righteousness sweep across our nation!

DAY FOUR

"Do not forsake wisdom, and she will protect you; love her, and she will watch over you." –Proverbs 4:6

Proudly watching over New York Harbor and the nation, stands the majestic Statue of Liberty. Liberty is portrayed in this statue and elsewhere as a lady. Such a precious commodity as liberty is rightly given human attributes. It is fascinating that the book of Proverbs does a similar thing with wisdom. Wisdom too, is called a lady, and is portrayed with human characteristics.

In the above passage from Proverbs, Lady Wisdom promises to protect and watch over us. It is a promise given with a condition. We must first choose to love wisdom and not forsake her. Thus embraced, wisdom will bring protection and watch care over a people.

Biblically speaking, wisdom is looking at things from God's perspective and making the right choices based on that perspective. How critical it is for a nation that wants to experience God's protection to love and embrace wisdom! As the United States increasingly accepts a secular mindset and rejects divine revelation as a basis for our laws, we move farther away from the protection offered by wisdom.

PRAYER POINTS

- Thank God for the gift of wisdom, and for the ability to see things from His perspective as we turn to His Word.
- Repent on behalf of our nation, because we have turned from making Scripture the basis of law, leaving behind wisdom, and looking to ourselves for truth.

• Cry out to the Lord, asking for godly wisdom to be loved and embraced once again by this nation.

My Prayer

I thank You, Lord, that You are a God of wisdom and revelation. You do not hide wisdom from us, but rather have told us that we only need to ask and You will freely give it. So, Father, we ask You for wisdom this day. We embrace the wisdom from above that allows us to see matters from Your perspective.

What we ask for ourselves personally, we also ask for our nation. Forgive us, Lord, for turning from Your ways and the wisdom that is Your Word. Our country has sought wisdom and direction from polls and surveys and other nations rather than looking to You. We have called Your wisdom "myth" and have called that which is foolishness "wisdom."

DAY FIVE

"But those who hope in the Lord will renew their strength. They will soar on wings like eagles; they will run and not grow weary, they will walk and not be faint." –Isaiah 40:31

The promise of renewed strength makes this a favorite Bible verse for many. The picture of a soaring eagle brings hope to those who are weary. For many years now, another soaring eagle has brought hope to many. The picture of America as a soaring eagle, proud, fast, moving above the clouds, has captured the imagination of millions, both in the United States and around the world.

But note that our verse today likens the eagle to those who hope in the Lord. Is that a picture of the United States today? It's a question not just for our government, but for us as citizens. Where is our hope? Is it in whomever currently occupies the White House or Congress? Is it in our military or economic strength?

There is nothing sadder than a crippled eagle, one that can no longer soar. Healing, however, can come to damaged wings. It involves the redirection of hope. The American eagle can soar again when we learn as a people to place our hope in the Lord.

PRAYER POINTS

• Thank the Lord how the biblical picture of a soaring eagle fits the symbol of our nation.
• Ask the Lord to help you put your hope and trust in Him alone.
• Pray for our nation, that we would once again soar as an eagle as we place our trust in the Lord.

My Prayer

Father, I thank You for this picture from the prophet Isaiah of an eagle soaring and how well that helps me as I pray for my nation today. Forgive us, Lord, for the pride that has often marked us a nation. That pride has caused us to put our hope in our own strength and might and not in You. Forgive us. If we are to run and not grow weary as a nation, it will be only because we have turned back to You as our hope. Help us, Lord, to hope in You!

DAY SIX

"Surely God is my salvation; I will trust and not be afraid. The LORD, the LORD, is my strength and my song; he has become my salvation." –Isaiah 12:2

T here are many things that can strike fear into the heart of a nation. In the years following the terrorist attacks of September 11, 2001, we have feared off-course planes, envelopes with white powder, and threats from extremists around the world. We take as many precautions as we can, all the while fearing that something, sometime will slip through and cause harm. Fear is tough to live with and causes a nation to react in manmade ways that are not always godly.

The Bible often warns us not to be afraid. The reason given is that God is our salvation. Salvation doesn't always refer to eternal life or heaven. It often means deliverance from the enemy. Psalm 32:7 says, "You are my hiding place; you will protect me from trouble and surround me with songs of deliverance." Isaiah reminds us that when a nation (or person) trusts in the Lord, He steps in and brings salvation. When we experience the Lord's deliverance, fear is replaced by songs of joy, as Isaiah declares in today's text. Has the Lord become your song?

PRAYER POINTS

• Bring your fears to the Lord and lay them at His feet.
• Ask the Lord to help the United States to learn to trust Him for our salvation as a nation.
• Confess (agree with God) that the Lord is indeed the salvation for our nation.

My Prayer

Lord, I agree with Your Word that You are our salvation. I believe that for my nation. Help us as a nation to cast aside fear and trust in You. Lord, do a mighty work in the hearts of Your people in the United States that brings about a national shift in priorities and confidence. We trust in You, Lord. Become our strength and our song!

DAY SEVEN

"Do not be afraid of them; the LORD your God himself will fight for you." –Deuteronomy 3:22

Yesterday's devotion also addressed the vital topic of national fear. Fear can paralyze a nation, or cause it to react in inappropriate ways. President Franklin Roosevelt understood that. When addressing a nation mired in the Great Depression, he reminded the people that the only thing they had to fear was fear itself. God gives us a very direct command when faced with enemies: "Do not be afraid of them." Don't give in to fear!

There is a very real reason why Israel in Moses' day was commanded not to fear. God Himself had promised to step in and fight on their behalf. They still had many battles ahead of them, but God had agreed to intervene in those battles for them. This promise can only be appropriated when a nation has committed itself to honor God and follow His ways. Wouldn't it be great to live in a nation that had so aligned itself with the purposes of God that we could live without fear because God had determined to fight on our behalf?

PRAYER POINTS

- Ask the Lord to pour out a spirit of repentance on our nation that we might become a nation committed to following His ways.
- Ask the Lord to help the United States to so line up with God's purposes that He will choose to fight on our behalf.
- Stand in prayer against all fear, whether in your own life or in the life of our nation.

My Prayer

Father, we turn from fear and turn to You. We indeed have enemies as a nation who seek our destruction. We have attempted to stand against them in our own strength, all the while rejecting Your lordship over us. Forgive us, Lord. Heal our land. Help us to turn back to You, so that You Yourself will fight for us.

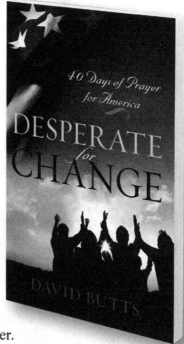

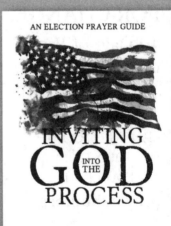